Change is Inevitable Growth is Optional

Learnings from Navigating Adversity

TROY J. COOK

outskirts press

Table of Contents

ONE

Diagnosis. At Last

"This is Troy."

"Troy, this is Dr. Smith."

"Yes, how are you today?"

"I am okay. Do you have a minute to talk?"

"Yes."

"No, Troy. I mean, do you really have a minute? I need your undivided attention."

"Okay."

"There is no easy way to tell you this, but I want to be completely upfront with you. After just a short time of reading your test results, the radiologists were able to make a confident and complete interpretation of your (dopamine transporter) DAT scan. Troy, you have young-onset Parkinson's disease. I wanted you to know as soon as I and the other doctors agreed to the diagnosis."

Silence . . .

"Troy, are you okay?"

Change is inevitable, growth is optional. Easy for me to type on the page and put into print. Kind of catchy. Almost a little sappy. Definitely meaningful.

Change is all around us every day. No one moment is the same as the one before or the one after. If only we could freeze time to the exact moment that was each of our visions of perfection. Now that would be great. That is not reality, and quite frankly, that is boring, simplistic, and naive.

As change occurs in each of our professional and personal lives, it is usually incremental and often not noticed in a significant way. We each make a set of instant split-second decisions on how to handle the constantly changing world. Our reactions to everything around us are mostly intuitive and unconscious. When a driver in front of us suddenly brakes, we let off the accelerator and cover our brake (or at least we were trained to do that at some point in time). These types of quick and intuitive reactions to change often fall into the categories of personal safety, survival, or what many refer to as natural.

But when the basic premises and assumptions in personal and professional life are not as we had planned, how do we react to those changes? Sales slump, your 401(k) goes down, a car needs replaced, divorce, a fire at a business, the best salesperson quits to join a competitor, and the list goes on.

Does the change engulf us into a fraction of what we were before? Do goals and priorities get set aside for basic survival mode? As our bodies changes over time—trust me, for those who are young and invincible, it will change—do we accept the "new you" and improve upon it? Thought-provoking and difficult questions for any of us or any business.

In any situation we face in life, there is always an option to grow from the change. Now this may sound altruistic. Maybe even not embedded in reality to some. However, we constantly hear stories of individuals who have traumatic events occur and how they deal with them. The most inspiring and impactful stores are those where the main characters find a path to grow on the back side of adversity. Within a business or organization, finding growth can be a tougher path. There are many characters with several story lines. Organizations with a specific defined purpose may not exist when their defined purpose is no longer needed. For example, the newspaper industry would argue the internet and other technology was not a change that allowed them to find a pattern of long-lasting growth. Sometimes the ever-changing business world creates the extinction of an industry. Often, however, businesses and individuals alike can find growth in the change, exploring new paths to carry out their mission.

Now it would be really great if each change faced in the world were easy to define. If only the path to growth from each change were clear and concise to follow. Or would it not be great if someone could write a book to show each of us how simple and easy it is to find growth. Then we move forward without having to think at a deep level, just intuitive reactions every time! A well laid out path for every occasion. I am sure there are such books. This is not one of those books. I am not going inform readers of how I survived a horrific event. Nobody will be able to exactly copy my every step and action to successfully do it just like I did! I did not make millions of dollars finding some system for how each reader can get rich quickly. Nothing against those books, as they are inspirational to many.

Each of us and our occupational pursuits are different and unique. Carpenters, surgeons, sales professionals, nurses, bankers, plumbers—no matter what your chosen field, our paths are distinctively different. Within each occupation, each person's journey is different. We are each on a different and unique journey. Our DNA is ours, whether we like it or not. How each of us react to the situations in life presented to us is also within our control. I wish I did not have Parkinson's Disease starting in my 40s. Seems really unfair, disappointing, and confusing. I have asked to trade with others who don't have my burden, but apparently those are options only available within a Hollywood script. Darn! Or maybe a movie script is in the works? Stay tuned.

There is good news to this whole premise of each of us being unique. We each also get to define our own path in life. The changing path could move forward on a road that looks like a dirt path. It may have unfilled holes and a creepy old, haunted house at the end. We may not like it, but it is our path. Who knows, maybe the creepy old house has an eccentric multimillionaire living in the basement. He has finished the remodeling of the perceived less than adequate shack as a sophisticated hangout complete with every modern technology. And when we knock on his door, he realizes how much he just wants to be loved and extends an invitation into his world. Next, as his best friend, he gives his millions of dollars to us fulfilling our every hope and dream! Or it could just be a rat- and raccoon-infested, dangerous old shack that requires it to be torn down, the remains burnt, and a new beginning for the lot where the house once stood.

Either ending to the dirt road analogy requires a similar journey or process to understand the needed steps to move forward. The process for identifying the change and establishing the pathway for growth is similar for all of us, no matter what our DNA. In listening to multiple stories of success from individuals and organizations, a similar process or system of defining growth and success becomes common. Each story ending is unique, but there are common threads to each successful journey. That is what this book is about … helping identify those common steps to embracing the constant change of life and then moving forward with choosing to grow from each change.

I have always believed growth was an option in the face of the most radical and abrupt changes. However, as stated earlier, that notion of a path of growth was deeply and abruptly challenged for me on July 13, 2017. At the moment a doctor informed me the last few years of my increasingly challenging life was part of a new state of being called Young Onset Parkinson's puts a new spin on "finding growth." Of course, I was shocked, angry, confused, depressed, and concerned. But I was also relieved to know what was now in front of me. And over the course of time, I began to embark on the same process I had previously identified, communicated to others, and engaged in with so many other situations in life. I had witnessed others, and experienced myself, the often-unconscious steps of moving forward each day to find growth. It has now become clear to me the education, experience, and information accumulated from others would provide me the best path forward to dealing with this abrasive and life-altering change. Those many stories of success came from both within organizations and from individuals, all helping to define a process to be applied to dealing with the inevitable change of life. I would choose and find a path of growth from change.

The following chapters outline the highlights of this process. Not only from my perspective of having Parkinson's, but also the stories of so many other organizations and people I have had the pleasure of listening to and experiencing. Often, the names of people and organizations have been changed to either protect their anonymity or to avoid having to share any royalties with them! (Hopefully you will be able to see the dry humor included throughout this book. If not, relax. Life is too short to be so uptight.)

TWO

Be Sure of the "Change"

Let's talk about green-ink pens. Yes, using a pen is almost a lost art, but follow the green-ink pen story anyway. Many people reading this book, or at least the first few chapters before getting bored and finding a different book, have likely never used a green-ink pen. Almost nobody uses a green pen on a regular basis. It is used for audits, correcting papers by teachers, and other very specific uses. Most people don't pick up and write with a green-ink pen, especially on a day-to-day basis, as their pen of conscious choice, unless it is a last option.

Imagine when the pen company who only made green-ink pens found themselves with a tiny share of the total pen market. More incredible than that statement is if the company leaders wondered why their market share was so low. Their pen was state of the art, a real distinctive writing tool. They thought it was obvious their price point was not correct. Lower the price.

That did not work, so then it is time to get rid of the sales team and get great "closers" on the team. They will drive retailers to put the pens front and center in every store. Leaders now were confident they had the right product at the right price. This will be easy for a good salesperson. But once again, limited sales. To any reader of this book, the problem seems somewhat clear at this point. Green ink is just not a big market. However, this is the same process we all go through at various points throughout our personal and professional lives.

We all accept change is occurring either consciously or subconsciously. However, being able to identify the parameters of the change is more difficult. It is also the first recognizable landmark in the journey of establishing growth from the existing constant change around us. Please note, the words "problems" or "issues" were not in the previous few sentences. Yes, life is full of what we define as problems and issues. Change is a more inclusive term, as problems are often defined by a negative context. Change can occur in both a positive or negative perspective. Winning a large prize in the lottery is an exciting change. Losing your job is not as exciting, and some may say negative. Each of these changes brings with it the need to approach the change with a consistent method of identification.

The change can be an obvious event, such as winning the lottery. However, the event may not be the actual change or disruption to our current state of being. There are two key aspects to identifying change: understanding the true core of the change, and evaluation of the skill sets needed to properly identify all of the aspects and details of the change.

For those who use Microsoft operating systems on a computer there is a great analogy to highlight this process. When the operating system or computer does not seem to be operating at an optimal level, experts tell us to hit the Control, Alt and Delete keys at the same time, known as Ctrl+Alt+Del. This is sometimes known as a system pause. It serves as a reset of the current situation. Then we get the choice of items such as switching users, locking your system, signing out, or looking at the task manager.

If we compare this process to our own lives or businesses, it is likely understood why we will not spend much time on comparing switching users, locking, or signing out. For a business, signing out or locking the system is not a great choice. Those choices basically end this book at this point. "Change is tough, so just give up" does not seem like a good message. Basic science classes have taught us it not feasible to "switch users," or swap places with another. Although that may happen in movies, it it not the real world. Well, this leaves us with the "task manager." Hitting Ctrl+Alt+Del and navigating to the task manager is a great comparison for assessing change.

Often, we make split-second decisions using this analogy. When driving and not finding the desired location, often we start down a street and realize quickly there has been a mistake in judgement. We need to stop this path and find another. In the old days, being a male meant taking a quick look at the map, making a split-second decision, and then going another direction with the outward utmost certainty. All the while, the family along for the ride was looking at the map and wondering what new "shortcut" had just been created by the "man" in charge. If it was a female in need of directions back in the day, the more intelligent gender in this debate often stopped at the nearest gas station (yes, children, there were "gas stations" back in the day that only did car repairs and sold gas) and calmly explained the need for directions. Of course, the same female was often asking a man who usually explained it in terms of navigational directions such as east-northeast and then a quick turn northwest most likely with the hopes of creating more confusion. Eventually, we all had to make quick decisions to the changing journey we were on. Today, when lost on a geographic journey, we reach for the GPS on our phones. It tells us where we are going, and unless there is a recent closure or change in the streets, arrival is achieved within seconds or minutes of the estimated time. GPS makes those split-second decisions for us at every step. Great invention, but not completely relevant to the conversation of this chapter in the book. I just wanted to point out the use of paper maps and fathers being confused by those maps is no longer a thing. This also pays homage to my own father and leave it to the imagination of the reader as to whether I received first-hand experience of this "I am not really lost, just taking a short cut" phenomenon. No charge for this part of the book. . . I wrote these words for free!

Ctrl+Alt+Del and the task manager provide us with lots of information. We can readily evaluate which programs were running we did not know were doing so. Maybe even a program running in the background we had no idea what it is or the nature of its purpose. We could also observe a program supposed to be working and it says, "not running." Darn. I hate that "not running" thing. Here is another safety tip: don't kick, throw, destroy, or swear loudly at the computer and think the "not running" will turn to "running." After numerous calls with IT professionals from multiple companies, I can attest none of these actions lead to a "fix." Well, at least fixing the system. However, properly assessing the task manager is the process we go through daily in getting to the core of change. We will follow this analogy periodically throughout this book as a method to properly identify and deal with change.

Let's dive into "finding the core of change." What is the true fire of change, not just the spark igniting the fire? Some reading this may say a fire is not a fair comparison, as many problems or issues in life are not fires. True, especially when considering all those quick intuitive reactions to a constantly changing world. We are not discussing small insignificant changes such as the rain beginning and the reaction to reach for the umbrella instead of getting wet. Often, seemingly small and insignificant reactions to relatively simple events or changes can become larger, more intense problems or issues. Now if we reach for an umbrella and discovered there was not one present, shoved the person next to us to the ground, stole their umbrella, and discovered pleasure in this new form of behavior . . . that be an issue. But come on, we all know we have such funny and odd thoughts about outbursts seemingly making the world a fairer and righteous place to each of us. Luckily for all of us, there are ethics which kick in during those situations. Now, back to identifying the core of an change.

A small and insignificant spark can cause a significant reaction to a change in the world. The larger reaction is often viewed or identified as the significant "change", causing individuals or organizations to veer down a completely different path than they should. My green-ink pen company is a classic example of this happening to organizations daily. A decision was reached during business planning about green-ink pens not based upon market research or sound business practice. It was likely on a passion for a great pen the world should want to own. Unfortunately, the world is changing constantly, and it does not appear the presence of more ink pen choices is a logical plan. We all know this happens often in organizations. "If you build it, they will come," only worked for Kevin Costner in *Field of Dreams*. If you are not familiar with this reference, go to your local movie rental store, check it out, and watch it on your home VHS player. Oh, change and evolution is all around us! No such place as a movie rental store. Did each of us know it was going to be our last time in a video rental store? Did the need to stop going just happen? One would struggle to find historical text highlighting a grand celebration or mourning event marking the end of video stores. Feel free to send me corrections to this statement. It does raise interesting questions about intuitive reactions to change.

For more than 18 months from late 2015 until July 2017, I found myself in a steadily declining personal health situation. In late 2015, by most accounts, I was in great shape. I was having success professionally, enjoying life, watching my kids become successful adults, soon to be an empty nester with my wife. I had these and many other great aspects of life in front of me for years to come as I was only 46 years "young."

Over several weeks I began to have headaches; relatively minor, but nonetheless, constant. They were headaches directly on my temples. At times the headaches worsened, but always a steady nagging pain. Next came fatigue, which increased substantially after I was exercising. I was working out on a regular basis at this time and had been in pretty good shape for a 46-year-old bald guy with a homely-looking face.

Next came a lot of strange muscle twitches in my arms and legs, and a small tremor in my right hand. Then the leg pain and other body pain became more intense and chronic. My sleep was greatly altered. My feet felt like they were cramping for hours at a time—an issue I had been dealing with quite often in prior years. The pain in my feet was similar to the cramp many of us have experienced in the arch of our foot for a quick moment. Mine was lasting for up to 30 minutes at a time and often several times in a day.

There were changes happening in my body I couldn't explain. I could not understand the core of the change. This is the same decision we each face daily. It is part of plotting the journey of life. We must identify the change around us requiring a reaction. So far, the small incremental changes had forced me to take more acetaminophen, try to sleep more, and lay off some exercise that was causing too much pain. All natural and almost benign reactions to changes I was facing. Surely reaching out to an expert would help me identify the next steps along my path. It was time to go to the doctor. My Ctrl+Alt+Del was not providing the information needed to move forward. More information and knowledge were certainly needed, or the "Task Manager" needed an expert for interpretation.

My primary care doctor, Dr. J (not his real name or initial) and I had known each other for years. We even worked out at the same health club at one point and often talked while at the club. After a brief visit and physical examination, he decided it was best to refer me to neurology for a consultation. My mother has Multiple Sclerosis (MS) and the doctor questioned me about her journey. The symptoms I presented to Dr. J were not leading to a specific cause, so a second opinion from a more specific expert made sense. Now understand, at this point, I was adamant I did not have MS. My symptoms were not consistent with MS. My mother had managed her MS successfully for over 20 years at this point. My first visit to neurology would end up being a great life lesson.

Earlier I mentioned that part of understanding the core of a life change within ourselves or an organization is assessment of the needed skills or expertise. Then, identification of the presence of those skills is present within the team is needed. This leads to awareness of the core of such a disruptive change. Expertise comes in a lot of forms. However it arrives, it is vital in identifying the root cause of change.

In my case, I am not a medical professional. Now I have been in health care, employee benefits, and insurance my entire career. At this point in my life, I worked with over 200 nurses and doctors. One great quality of medical professionals is when asked, they will give you an opinion. One troubling issue with medical professionals is when asked, they will give you an opinion. My medical professional colleagues understand the fact that without great knowledge of the individual circumstances, opinions are just suggestions to talk to your own medical professional about. Doctors and nurses are careful to not over diagnose. For this, we should all be grateful, as they are aware of the complexity of the human body and difficulty of diagnosis. If only all people would have the same approach to providing their "expertise" to those around them that may or may not ask for their unqualified and unsolicited opinion.

Assessing the skill set need to completely identify the aspects of significant change is complicated and tricky. It requires the realization a person or organization may not have the proper skills to identify root causes of change on their own. Being sick is not a good example, as most know a medical professional is needed in times of great health stress. For other issues, such as personal finance, college choice, or sales team evaluation, we often make the mistake of thinking we are the expert. Please note: anyone who does not have a sound process and specific metrics for establishing why they are an expert, is not a likely candidate to be included on any team, anywhere, ever.

When Ctrl+Alt+Del is used, and the programs showing up on the task list are not programs recognizable, that should be the signal to find help now! So, please…Find help!!

The most successful individuals and organizations create a process to identify and understand the parameters of the evolving world their business functions within. *Metrics* seems to be an overly used term these days, but having a process for evaluation is key. Without a process or system, reactions to change are not grounded in logical, long-term priorities. The chosen path or response to the change may be right, or then again it may lead to an unknowing random path going nowhere. In essence, those with a process for evaluation hit Ctrl+Alt+Del to understand the programs and processes working, programs and processes not running well, and those seeming to just be opened. Often there are functions, programs, processes, or protocols that are just open and not tied to a specific goal. These typically equate to a function just being performed for the sake of completion with no intentional or needed impact to the business.

Between the time I was referred to and the actual visit with my first neurologist, whom I will call Dr. X (it will soon be clearly understood why his name is protected), I had a few other issues of concern. Those included one very interesting issue in that I fell one morning trying to get dressed. Lost my balance and went face first on the carpet. Not a big deal, as I must have going too fast.

Of course, I mentioned each of the symptoms to Dr. X. Before I could even get most of them out, he stopped me. He said he saw in my family history my mother has MS. I confirmed that fact. After I informed him I did not think I had this, he moved on. Little did I know he and my primary care doctor had put in their notes a statement I could not get past with other physicians for quite some time. They believed it was likely I was suffering from worry and anxiety about having inherited MS from my mother and the other symptoms were not related or psychosomatic.

Dr. X made his original diagnosis with limited physical testing and no diagnostic testing. It was clear to him; I was not drinking enough water during workouts. To make this problem go away I should use a sports drink during exercise. He said the headaches were "rebound headaches" from too much acetaminophen. I learned most physicians will argue there is not an actual diagnosis or condition called "rebound headaches." His remedy for sleep and the headaches was to give me a sedative at night so I could get sleep. This would relieve the headaches as I would be getting the proper rest and recovery.

During this time, I also suffered from unique physical symptoms called mesenteric infarctions. In essence, small blood clots in my abdomen. Now nobody should worry I was in jeopardy of having a clot move to the brain or heart. These types of clots are small and can't travel out of the mesentery lining of the abdominal area. However, I would come to find out later they were likely caused by swelling and a slowing of my intestinal tract often caused by Parkinson's. I can attest to the swelling and slowing. Both are painful. These infarctions were discovered by my primary care doctor as he consulted another specialist physician on the first infarction that was picked up from a CT scan. I had gone into Dr. J with an extremely painful abdomen. The decision was made to do nothing about this discovery as it was likely not of concern unless the pain persisted. The pain did get better, but only for a brief period. The second infarction sent me to the ER. It was more painful.

The same process identified the infarction and there was a decision to monitor this situation going forward. Eventually, these infarctions became a significant piece of information in identifying my disease state, albeit much later. Of course, it is easy to look back and second guess the process.

After two follow-up visits with the first neurologist, the infamous Dr. X, and no progress on my symptoms, he came to a conclusion. He insisted, "there is no neurological issue with you." I was sent back to primary care in November of 2016.

After a plea with Dr. J, my primary care doctor, he ran blood tests. Good news. The blood tests showed results we could begin to use as a path forward. Bad news . . . I had a high SED rate and had a positive auto-immune (AA). SED rate is from swelling in the body. That would make sense. I had also gained about 20 pounds from lack of exercise due to pain and fatigue. The AA factor was an indication of potential items in the auto-immune and Lupus family of disorders and diseases. Not a potentially fun diagnosis.

Two weeks later, we entered a rheumatology office. He quickly ruled out Lupus and started treating me for chronic centralized pain, or centralized pain syndrome (CPS). As we have learned thus far in this book, I was diagnosed with Parkinson's. However, the diagnosis of CPS was not wrong. It was just not the core change. As it turns out, the CPS diagnosis was a further piece of information in reaching the exact and specific core of the change.

As mentioned earlier, having the right team of experts in place is a necessary part of the process. Clearly my rheumatologist was taking action and he started me on a drug regimen. Clearly Dr. X, the neurologist, was not taking me down a path of successful recognition of the root cause of the change. It is nobody's fault, as he was not the right fit for building my successful team.

Again, finding the root of a problem often takes a team of experts. It may just be two people, but two do make a team. At this point of my journey, my team of experts was myself and the rheumatologist. A team of two.

If we circle back to our Green Pen Company example from earlier, it is clear the many actions the green pen company took did not solve their issues. It is also clear if they truly hit Ctrl+Alt+Del, they did not identify the tasks needed to understand the problem or life change they were embedded in. Remember, recognizing the problem may often require specific expertise and analysis. Green Pen Company did not have the right team members at the table, or they did not have a system to measure success. Maybe the most troubling would be they did not have the right team members or have a system. Massive corporate failures are often examples of both. With a lack of any process or system, failing organizations don't recognize the root cause and often blame individuals. I see this most often with those who are in sales positions.

Sales is a tough field; we would all agree. There are often many factors impacting whether a specific salesperson has success with any one prospective customer or client. At Green Pen, they did not measure sales activity as specifically as they measured manufacturing or accounting. The sales process is not always about the final sale. A salesperson can't sell a product nobody wants. Green Pen asked consumers to buy a product that only a few consumers wanted to own. Especially in a changing world with technology driving the market, the company did not successfully understand the root of their problems. As well, they set no path forward based upon creditable evidence from a qualified team. And it is easy to blame the target for what is toughest to measure . . . sales.

There have been many leaders and organizations who thought the lack of sales was a sales problem before they actually began to assess how they were measuring sales. They looked at only the end result. However, measuring the entire process of selling can often identify if the problem is an individual issue or a process issue. If the sales team is meeting the established metrics of contacts to the market and nobody is purchasing, there are likely other issues existing apart from the people assigned to sell.

Identification of the problems or issues and the root causes is key to understanding the changes constantly bombarding us. Our innate ability to hit Ctrl+Alt+Del is key in assessing and managing a defined and specific process or system of recognition. Occasionally, there is a big spark that lights a fire. The wild flames of a fire are clearly presenting a big change. The change can still be just that, a change. It may be positive or negative, but it will have impact upon an individual or organization's set of goals and priorities. However, the primary attention often is focused on the spark lighting the elements already present for a fire or change.

THREE

⚮

2 Minutes and 13 Seconds

When I received the call from Dr. Smith, my second neurologist, informing me of the Parkinson's diagnosis, I felt as if the world was standing still. I knew a call would come at some point informing me of the test results. But not at that specific moment. I had a "feeling" or suspicion there was not good news coming, but hearing the words was alarming and deafening to all other happenings in the world. It was a large identifiable spark, lighting a smoldering fire of change.

The phone call lasted 2 minutes and 13 seconds. Exactly 2:13. But as with any situation where the world is suddenly changing in front of us, the perception of time is distorted and altered. Why? There are many complex psychological and physical reasons we could analyze to answer the reason why time plays tricks on our minds. The commonsense reason for this bizarre distortion of time we experience is factual. We perceive our worldview is changing. What we perceived as normal and status quo is now challenged down to our fundamental beliefs. Anyone who says they have not experienced this, is either completely without emotion or has no life beliefs or goals. If an organization has not experienced this, they are either too new or their true passion for a mission and vision is not strong enough to elicit emotional response.

We all know where we were when certain historical events occurred. I was in elementary school when Ronald Reagan was shot. I went home and watched the live coverage on one of my few channels on TV for hours. It was the first time I had experienced such an event in my lifetime. Taking out the inherent political bias built into our current American culture today, the news of this type of event was shocking, scary, and caused Americans to pause. The President had just been shot! I had read about such an event most definitely. Heard my parents talk about such jaw dropping moments; of course. But actually deciphering the words our teachers told us, "The President has been shot," was a new and confusing feeling I was experiencing for the first time. My parents had lived through the Kennedy shootings and the attempt on President Ford's life. Once it became evident President Reagan was going to survive, my parents already lower level of anxiety than mine completely diminished. Their worldview had not changed. It was not a Soviet attack, or a terrorist attack, and their world order was still in place.

When each of us experiences such an event for the first time there are different and new iterations of feeling and emotions. Winning a championship or contest nobody from the school or team has ever won; launching a new product line which immediately takes off; saving or propelling a company to new heights; placing the final piece of steel in place on the core structure of the tallest building in the city. These are all events accompanied by emotions, memories, lifelong scenes of reenactment in our minds, and often move us in new directions or provide increased focus on a chosen path of success. The actual event is typically and often not as significant as we remember it to be. Or the specific long-term effects of such an event on a community or society are difficult to define. The immediate and long-term emotional impressions we have in our minds are likely the result of our own personal record button. That recording is embedded within the private movie reel of our life experiences.

At organizations and companies, these images are often captured in historical documents and photos to be relived at appropriate times. Over time, those who were not part of those events become a majority of team members. Thus, the sense of enormous pride or anxiety for the change decreases for those particular sparks and memories. The effects of the change often remain but with limited understanding of the specific events and circumstances around the events. The choice the company made remains: to accept change and move through a journey not of their choosing, or to embrace the change and find their own path of growth. The same is true for each of us in the world.

My 2:13 event did not take just 2:13 seconds. July 13, 2017, was the date of the spark, not the entire event. During the spark of 2:13, I had to begin making conscious decisions of how I would embrace my new world. Looking back on the details of the day and the entire event the day sparked, the identification of the spark and the event are undisputed facts.

As previously noted, I had been to numerous doctors and

had numerous tests. Here are the exact numbers as best as I can put them together. During the 18 months prior to July 13, I had 6 major blood draws with multiple vials of blood taken each time, one brain MRI (luckily, they actually found I had a brain), three CT scans, two mesenteric infarctions (at least they know of), four different physicians treating me, and hundreds of opinions from family, friends, and other medical professionals I ran into. Okay, I should not have been completely caught off guard if there was a change happening in my life! Keep in mind, all these events and the accompanying symptoms were over at least 18 months. It was only in the last three to five months prior to diagnosis I could sense the change.

In January of 2017, when the rheumatologist met with me for an update on the pharmacy cocktail he'd prescribed in December, we discussed the little, if any, improvement in my symptoms. In fact, it seemed worse. Headaches increased, pain the same, tremor still noticeable, fatigue growing, strange cramps in my feet. However, the decision was made to continue the course. There had not been enough time on the current path to make a clear determination of success or failure. And I thought of it as success or failure. Not treatment, maintenance, or control. It was win or lose. For those in sales, it was making the sale, or they say no. I had someone who attended a speech I gave on this subject tell me, "You build the wall or it does not exist. There is no in between or half-built." I was beginning to experience this sense of all or nothing in my journey. At this point, it was feeling like a loss.

A few months later, my wife and I both attended the follow-up visit at rheumatology. At that time, I was traveling for my job about 50 percent of the time. East to west, north to south. Name a place - I had likely been there or close by in the last 24 months. I was able to hide many of my symptoms from close family and friends, as I was by myself quite often. So, when my wife asked to attend the follow-up rheumatology appointment with me, it could have been because she greatly missed me. Not likely, as I am a pain in the butt to live with on a normal basis. At his point in my life, I was unbearable. She must have been very concerned.

This entire period of time I was dealing with these conditions, I often fought off the notion I was "just being dramatic." Early on in my journey to diagnosis, I had people close to me roll their eyes when I did finally share my not feeling well. Most of the time they were unaware they were doing it. I believe human nature to be one of two courses when presented with such news as I was sharing of discomfort and concern for my health. Either individuals get overly concerned or they think nothing of it. There is seldom a middle ground, in my experience. Much of our personal reaction to adverse news such as I was sharing is likely based upon our own experiences in life. This response mostly becomes an automated response. I rarely took offense to those who rolled their eyes or who became disinterested. Even when they had started the conversation with, "Are you feeling okay, you don't look yourself." When I shared, I was not well, then they would shut down. We all do this as hearing bad or negative news is troubling. It is a human reaction.

Keep in mind, I have not been short on medical trauma, drama, and interesting scenarios. Here are the events all before sixth grade. I fell off a slide as a kid and suffered a likely severe head injury, got my head smashed against a cement pool edge on vacation in the Ozarks with a big lump to follow and likely mild concussion, I suffered from mild childhood asthma and allergies which I grew out of in puberty.

But the fun does end in sixth grade. Before my seventh-grade year, doctors discovered a hydrocele in my right testicle. It was a scary surgery, and I was not aware of the potential for the tumor to be malignant. Doctors came two weeks later to inform my parents it was benign and I now understand how concerned they must have been. Thank you to my parents for sheltering me from that fear as it made that period much easier. Then while in seventh grade I bruised my tailbone severely and smashed up my elbow sledding. Eighth grade saw me break my wrist, which still causes me problems today. In ninth grade I tore up my shoulder (which eventually resulted in surgery as an adult), burned my lungs running outside in the extreme cold, and pulled a groin muscle, causing swelling to a level not so cool for a 15-year-old boy. A series of sprained ankles through-out high school, with what we now know was one broken ankle at the time (maybe should have gone to the doctor instead of just "tapping it up"). There were also more shoulder problems, two more concussions, and a horrific hurdling accident that ripped up my neck and back for years.

In college, I was diagnosed with mild Crohn's disease. I was treated for three or four mild attacks over several years. For the last 15 or so years, doctors think my Crohn's was either never really Crohn's (medical technology was not as good in 1988 as it is now) or I am one of a small group of folks who had a complete remission.

But wait . . . it gets better. My close friends love the follow-ing analysis, or at least it gives them great material for comic relief. In all, I have had 12 surgeries, have 22 (I think) inci-sions on my body, broke my left wrist twice, each ankle once, and had multiple concussions. My friends joke with me at how I am even holding together. One can only imagine what to think when I start informing others of all the symptoms I was having prior to the Parkinson's diagnosis. They may not have been as concerned as they should have. Based upon my past, I completely understand. My medical history is a lot to take in for a medical professional. It is a little overwhelming for a non-medical professional who is not being paid to treat me.

However, some in the medical community were not taking my current symptoms as serious as would have hoped, as mentioned in chapter two. But now my wife was wanting to be with me on this follow-up visit. This should have been another glaring siren of pending problems. My wife's comment to the rheumatologist went something like this: "This is not my husband; he is nothing close to what he was a year ago. The drugs are not working, and he is declining steadily." Looking back, that day was a clear beginning of me having to define a new path in my journey in life.

The tremors had definitely worsened, although I was hiding it well. This precipitated a referral to Dr. Smith, the best movement disorder specialist in Des Moines, according to my doctor. But my rheumatologist said, "I believe this is just an essential, benign tremor. However, we should rule out other causes." Remember, he was also reading a file from my primary care doctor and first neurologist that indicated I was just suffering from anxiety and was more of a hypochondriac. Off we went to Dr. Smith in June of 2017.

Dr. Smith was clear and concise with me. She asked me about my fears of MS and could I be imagining symptoms. Again, I stated I had never thought I had MS. Wow, how one poor medical opinion can dog your files forever. She ordered two significant tests, a DAT scan, and an MRI of the brain. With my travel schedule and testing schedule, we did not get them booked for completion until July 15 and 16. By this time, it was clear there was an underlying issue beyond just centralized pain syndrome as I had been diagnosed. Close friends and family were noticeably concerned. I could see it and feel it.

This is not unlike any significant change in each of our lives or the life of an organization. I think back to a story shared to me by a former high school football coach I spent time with. Coach M, as I will call him, is an amazing man. He coached high school football for decades, was a golf coach for years, and an activities director. All of this at the same high school he attended as a student. A dedicated father, husband, and pillar of a community which relied upon him in many ways. He relayed many nuggets of wisdom and amazing stories in my time with him. One of those stories was about his decision to become an associate principal and activities director.

In the prime of Coach M's high school coaching career, he felt a lack of passion for his work. He was not slacking off by any means, but the day to day work had become more of grind than in the past. He wasn't sure why, as he was leading a perennial power in their class in football each year, he was a beloved physical education teacher, and he had a good life by all accounts. He had offers from a few businesses to leave coaching and certainly make a great deal more money. However, those did not have significant interest for him.

Then came a change in the administration in his high school. Suddenly, he saw a different path. A path to grow into a new role. He became a half-time administrator and half-time teacher. It was perfect for him. He conveyed to me how his attention to detail and passion for football became greater than he could have imagined. He was choosing to find growth. He went on to win a state title in football and would coach numerous college players. His coaching tree has on it an amazing number of coaches branching out from him. Many of those coaches going onto become mentors and sharing their passion for coaching with the next generation. That coaching tree and legacy still runs deep throughout his state. If he had not chosen to find the opportunity to grow in the face of the changing world around him, there would have been a smaller ripple effect for generations to come. Change is inevitable, growth is optional.

As evidenced by the path I was on, the 2:13 call should not have been a complete surprise. I was in the midst of a big life change. The week of my diagnosis was a sobering time, even prior to hearing the final verdict. On Monday of that week, I went in for a brain MRI. Now, if one has not had to slide into a long tube headfirst, sounding like a jet engine revving up and filling the body with radiation, one has not truly lived. For those who have had such an experience, now imagine it while having right hand tremors with little predictability of onset. This was a fabulous experience. I was already nervous and starting to feel anxious about my week of testing. Anxiety and uncontrolled tremors are not formula for a smooth MRI experience. They slid me into the tube, scanned me, slid me out, injected me with contrast, and slid me back in again. In all, about 45 minutes of fun. Luckily the great techs and the soft music on the headphones were enough to get me through. Credit should also go to the wash cloth I was allowed to have under a death grip. The cloth assisted me in controlling the tremor and torso movement I had developed to counter tremors.

Then on Tuesday morning, the day after my MRI, I reported to a different testing center for a test called a DAT scan. It was described to me as a conclusive test for Parkinson's. DAT

Scans are almost perfect with a positive diagnosis but do have a potential for false negative test results. Dr. Smith and my wife both told me I would need to accept the results of this test, no matter the result. There was again doubt in the voices of those around me.

This doubt from many of the team members began to occasionally affect me. I was starting to doubt the presence of the many symptoms I was working through. Essentially, I began hiding many signs of my Parkinson's. I did not know it was Parkinson's at this point, so I was not recognizing the combination of the many symptoms. If I had not engaged in this self-doubt, there may have been a quicker diagnosis. Then again, it would not have been helpful for the medical team to have all of the knowledge and information they needed to make an informed diagnosis. Hopefully we can all see the ridiculousness of my last sentence. Having all the facts is seldom, if ever, an impediment to wise decisions. Unfortunately for me, at this point of the process, there was only limited recognition by me or my team we were in the midst of extreme negative adversity. This lack of recognition was causing gaps in the diagnosis process.

Now this DAT scan test was more than a little scary. It began with a wonderful small cocktail of contrast. After an hour, then there was an injection of a radioactive substance nothing short of a concoction one would see a mad scientist laboring over with a smile. I was told the substance has to be injected within 24 hours of being prepped or it is wasted. Exactly the kind of substance we all desire to have a lab tech inject in the body. It was more reassuring when the tech wore thick gloves and a mask when she took the substance out of the cooler.

After the injection, I had to wait three hours, I believe. I left the clinic, went to a local coffee shop, worked on my computer and returned phone calls. During my time at the coffee shop, a disturbing phone call came in. It was Dr. Smith calling to inform me of my MRI results from the day before. She was clear with me on the results. Doctors considered the images to be unremarkable.

There was one exception to the "unremarkable" comment. They did find three small spots appearing to be caused by trauma. They were all in insignificant locations for indication of Multiple Sclerosis. There is no MS. Wow! It might have been mentioned prior in this book, but just in case, I will say it again. There was little or no signs of MS and I did not think I had MS.

I likely should have mentioned earlier in this story, but an MRI can't diagnose Parkinson's. It can only rule out other neurological diseases. Parkinson's is characterized by a lack of dopamine in your brain. Dopamine is a significant neurotransmitter in the brain connecting one's nerves and muscles. It allows for smooth muscle movement, the ability to fight pain, and other smaller functions. Keeping in mind the body is full of nerves and muscles, dopamine is significant for leading a "normal" existence. Those with Parkinson's have at least an 80 percent reduction of their dopamine level. The dopamine in your brain is not replaceable. Once it is gone, well . . . Parkinson's. More on the disease itself later in this book.

The news from Dr. Smith was more than interesting. Those few spots were likely caused by concussions. I have had more damage to brain in the form of a concussion than one should be exposed to. She asked me to think about connecting with my parents to put together the details of my concussions, as they occurred while I was in school. She mentioned the possibility of the MRI images being related to the early signs of CTE, chronic traumatic encephalopathy. This potential diagnosis was starting to make sense to me, as I was familiar with it. Being a former football player and coach, I had a limited working knowledge of CTE. This potential was also very scary. There is not a definitive test to diagnose CTE except with an autopsy, meaning after death. However, the medical community is recognizing the symptoms more clearly today with appropriate treatment plans to manage the effects. This was potential game changing news from Dr. Smith.

Dr. Smith and I finished the conversation with her asking about how the prep was going for my DAT scan. She politely reminded me the reading of the scan by radiology usually takes 48–72 hours. She continued to explain this complicated DAT Scan test and the few radiologists in the metro area who were extremely proficient with this scan. I called my wife immediately after finishing with Dr. Smith to provide the update and we began to think about CTE.

The DAT scan itself was not a great experience. It was less intimidating than the MRI but hardly a great runner-up. The head is strapped down so it does not move back and forth, up or down, or in my case, no tremor. The head tremor was also now a small symptom I noticed. Especially at night, I was experiencing a little head shaking. During this test there is also no sneezing or coughing. The camera sits just an inch or two from the head, slowly rotating around the entire strapped-down head while lying on a narrow, uncomfortable board. At least it was over.

As most know, radiology techs are instructed to never indicate any potential results they may be seeing. However, when I completed my test and was getting unstrapped, the tone of the conversation with my tech was different than before we started the test. She tried to hide the fact she had seen something disturbing, but clearly, she did not want to talk. This lack of talking was completely different than while she was strapping me down for the ride. There was not the normal conversation and "I hope you enjoy your day here at the amusement park." She had seen the images indicated I had a greatly diminished supply of dopamine. She knew where this was going and was trying not to tip her hand. She saw me off with final instructions the doctor would call me in 48–72 hours. Again, the spark for my life change was just starting to be lit. All the indication lights were now starting to go off, but I was not seeing them completely . . . yet.

The next day changed my awareness of imminent change. It's late Wednesday morning and I am just getting dialed into a webinar, when my cell phone rings. I answered and the conversation I started this book with unfolds. Two minutes and 13 seconds. I had been diagnosed with Parkinson's at the age of 48 and had likely had it for quite some time.

As I mentioned earlier, time has a way of standing still when the spark of change lights the fire with an explosion. I called my wife, who was still at home and told her to stay there. I said I'd heard from the doctor and was on my way home. I told my team members in the office I was going to the doctor as there was an issue I needed to follow up on.

Now here is one of the amazing parts of this. When my wife asked me a couple hours later how long I had been on the phone with the doctor, I told her about 10 minutes, maybe longer. Actual time according to my cell phone records, well, we all know; 2 minutes, 13 seconds. Time had stood still. Most every part of my world quickly played out in my mind, and it felt like at least 10 minutes had passed.

There is more to this story. If anyone is freaked out by strange and unusual circumstances or think there is a hidden supernatural or God-like meaning to such situations, this may be the time to move onto the next chapter of this book. What I am about to say will certainly make everyone think about supreme intervention. I still get chills when I think about it, talk about, or as I write about. Each time I have read this section of the book for editing and rewriting, I still pause to think more deeply than the time before. So here it is.

I have been blessed to speak around the country on various topics including keynote presentations about success and life fulfillment. Until I decided to get Parkinson's (yes that is a very sick form of humor), I prided myself on telling stories of others almost all of us could relate to. I had not ever talked much about myself. I love being on stage and communicating with an audience. It is maybe the only talent I have—relating to audiences and conveying a message. I get excited and inspired every time I am asked to speak, prepare to speak, and actually do the presentation.

Shortly after being diagnosed with Parkinson's, I mentioned my diagnosis in a presentation to a small group. Much to my surprise, they were spellbound by the topic. It had not occurred to me there would be such a reaction. It became clear this was a connection audiences wanted to hear about. I decided to ramp up my speaking. In the process of doing so, I thought the 2:13 change would be a great story to convey. The whole time standing still moment seemed to connect. Great dramatic effect! After discussing this with my wife, we started talking about a 2-minute-and-37 second conversation. That is the time we both remembered. We had looked at my cell phone and 2:37 was etched into our memories. However, we were wrong. I had already gone out and started talking about 2:37. Then my wife went back and looked up the exact call on my cell-phone record.

It was 2:13. Not a big deal. Think again, here's the odd part. My birthday is February 13th. Yes, 2/13! What prompted my lovely bride to look is unknown, but we had been wrong. I know it is just a coincidence, but I still get chills. Could have been 59 other numbers in that two-minute timeframe. It was not.

FOUR

COMMUNICATION
PLAN, PLEASE.

HOW DOES ONE tell their spouse they have been diagnosed with a life-altering, life-threatening, progressive neurological disease one is not sure how to define or describe?

Looking back, the 15-minute drive home after hearing news over the phone from my doctor, now to inform my wife, was all about assessing how this conversation would evolve. I suppose I could have stopped along the way and searched the internet for a quick read on how to handle such an easy situation. It is likely there is a how to guide for such a situation. Surely, the how to guide would have completely solved my problem. I had not been exposed to any such training or had to provide such an explanation prior in my life. There were previous experiences in my life of explaining to others how their lives were changing. Such as having to let go of an employee or other such event. Delivering such bad news as a Parkinson's diagnosis was foreign to me, as I was the one delivering bad news about myself.

Whenever we go through times of change, knowing how to communicate those changes is almost as important as the change itself. Of course, we all want to grow from any change, whether good or bad. Every company faces an evolving world, often causing a rapid and decisive correction in the journey of success. As an organization with employees, volunteers, and customers, a well-thought-out communication plan is often constructed by communication experts. These folks are invaluable to organizations. Any organization who thinks they can just "figure it out on their own," or "wing it and see what happens," is not living in reality. When a CEO communicates to employees, the relationship is unique, as it is from boss to employee. When a small not-for-profit is communicating with its volunteers, the relationship is not the same as boss to employee.

There are several examples of the differences in the framing and disseminating of significant messages. The best examples would show the distinct manners each communication plan was designed to reach the desired audiences successfully with efficiency and effectiveness. We all know miscommunication, as those are the examples we tend to remember the most. Often at the root of many relationship failures between coworkers, employees and employers, and companies and their consumers lie miscommunication that is almost always unintended.

As individuals, whenever we face life-altering situations, we communicate to our own teams of friends and family. Hopefully, if there is a slight miscommunication with family and friends, there is an opportunity to rectify the loss of trust, confusion, or anger. We have all been there. Hopefully we all have support systems around us providing grace to each of us in these times of unintended consequences.

There are commonalities to communicating significant change whether at an organizational or individual level. There are entire books written on this topic. Heck, you can get a college degree in such a topic. Of course, my communication specialist friends would ask for a reminder to readers of the difficult and complicated work their degree was, and their current jobs are! When battling the beginning of a significant change and seeking to grow from it, recognition of the scope of the situation and those impacted is one of the first steps in planning. Communicating news such as PD is fundamentally no different.

During the communication process of my Parkinson's diagnosis, another key aspect of planning the communication was reinforced. It is imperative to not just know who the audience is in name and description, but to understand the audience. One could argue it is a deep, multi-faceted understanding of the audience and is vital for planning. Recognition and understanding allows for genuine communication to the target audience. Additionally, this understanding and genuine communication will aid in defining which of those audience members will either continue to be a long-term relationship, the expansion of an existing relationship or the beginning of a new unforeseen relationship.

Earlier in this book, Coach M was discussed and his decision to move into an assistant principal role was highlighted. He is full of great life stories, as mentioned earlier. His ability to communicate with high school boys is an example for anyone, anywhere, anytime. We all understand high school boys are a unique specimen of human beings. Enough said about this fact, as having dealt with high school boys at any level is enough experience to support my factual assumption.

Coach M engaged in a unique and successful communication technique. Most days at the end of practice, Coach had the boys, soon to be men, take a knee (for those who don't know football coach language, that meant kneel on one knee; don't sit, don't stand, take off your helmet and kneel). Coach M had a list of topics he rotated throughout the football season for these end-of-practice discussion sessions. Each lasted three to five minutes and were delivered with specific intent. It did not matter if the practice was good, bad, hot, cold, after a win or loss, most practices ended with a life talk. These life lessons included topics such as treating members of the opposite sex with respect, respect for authority, love, family, and others of a similar nature. Sometimes they were interactive with one of his team captains or team leaders assisting him. Although the daily message varied, the overarching theme was clear: life is about more than football. What was learned in the preparation for each game was transferrable to life in a connection Coach helped the young men to understand. The respect his players had for him during and after their time as a player was unparalleled. He was not just their coach; he was a walking example of the many life lessons he shared.

His communication style with his players was fitting for the audience. He knew the proper balance of coach, father figure, friend, and mentor. If a parent had been waiting to talk to Coach M five minutes after practice, they did not receive the same message. He told me parents deserve to have their questions answered about their son in a direct, honest, and adult manner. He placed himself in their position as a parent and treated them with the respect they deserved. Most every parent would share the same sentiment about their experience. They never doubted their son would learn tremendously while on a Coach M team. He successfully created an intersection between football and life. Know the audience and communicate appropriately. It goes a long way.

Talking to a group of young football players is not the same as telling workers their division is being closed and they will lose their jobs. Nor is telling a group of volunteers their efforts raised record-breaking amounts for a charitable cause. They are unique groups, but the core approach should not be dissimilar. Knowing and deeply understanding the audience is always relevant to effective and honest communication.

Telling one's wife of 25 years, after having met her when at 18 years of age, doctors have provided a diagnosis of a disease that will likely steal the ability to spend the planned-on retirement with her may not appear in the same general vicinity of the examples above. It could also be assumed one could say telling friends and family of such news is again a unique situation. Let me throw another unique example. Communicating to parents a recent diagnosis of their youngest son with Parkinson's Disease.

While driving home immediately after my phone call with Dr. Smith to talk with my wife, I realized this was a difficult discussion. Providing the needed comfort to her from a confusing and scary diagnosis became a priority in my mind. My personality is to be a pleaser. I do this to a fault. I will push my belief of the correct route to endless happiness as often as I can. If anyone asks me to help, I will never leave them alone until I believe they have found my definition of contentment or happiness. Yes, I am aware of this character flaw.

In telling my wife the diagnosis, it was important to respect her feelings and emotions, while also looking for comfort for myself. This complex analysis I performed in my 15-minute drive led to pulling into the garage to find her with the house door from the garage open and her standing in it. She knew my frantic phone call telling her not to leave the house was not good. She stood there waiting, likely knowing there was bad news. I knew my approach, had even rehearsed it on my way home. My wife is a direct communicator in situations such as these. She wants to know the situation and facts completely. Then, she can process and begin the next steps in her mind. I got out of the car and walked up the three steps to the door.

"The doctor called. There is no doubt, it is Parkinson's." We hugged and I explained it took two radiologists less than two hours to read, confirm, consult with Dr. Smith, and send the report saying my results were consistent with Young Onset Parkinson's. Direct, to the point, and now we can move on. She wanted the news specifically that way. Looking back, I could not have communicated much better to her, or later to my children. But, of course, I understand their styles, making the first day the easiest day of communication there would be for the next several approaching weeks.

The next communications would not be as easy. This may be surprising, but I was familiar with my immediate family's communication styles and preferences. Of course, we had knowledge on many of our friends and family's preferences, but it is not as intuitive and conditioned into our daily routines. We needed a plan, just like any company or individual delivering news of this magnitude.

There were several questions to address. Who do we tell, if anyone? How do we tell each of them? Do we keep this to ourselves? We had friends, family, colleagues, and who could possibly know where the list would end. Each group would need a specific evaluation of the most effective communication plan. Heck, at this point I had not even been back in front of the doctor, but my mind was swirling. The next day was our follow-up appointment to review the details of the testing and receive a prognosis and treatment plan. There I was trying to figure out very specific steps before I even had all the needed information.

Here we were, July 12, 2017, about lunchtime. What does one do next when standing inside my house looking at my wife? Our relationship of 25 plus years was just thrown a nasty curve ball. The answer for us at that moment was easy. My wife and I went out for lunch, having a glass of wine with our food. We talked through a short-term game plan. Short-term was really just how to get through the next 36 hours. We weighed the options of the possible next steps and formulated the best plan we could for the next several hours. Then we laid out a tentative plan for the next several days, knowing the plan may need to be altered based upon our meeting with medical personnel the next day.

It is rare in life that we get to think through how to communicate a life-altering change as it is occurring. Many times, we are reacting and hoping our reactions truly reflect the message we wanted to or needed to communicate. A lack of communication can also be an issue. Although it may seem more thoughtful to show no reaction and communicate later to a situation or event, it can come across as insensitive, uncaring, or arrogant. Each of us can explain very specific examples of overcommunication and lack of communication causing a situation to be perceived as worse than the original event. The perception then can become the reality that has to be managed.

Having encountered many great leaders and outstanding people in my life, there is evidence each of those leaders has developed their own communication style and process. One common factor between all of them: they have trained themselves to react consistently with their own specific style for situations they encounter. Oh sure, the experts may advocate all communication should be situational. Those same experts may also assume any person can be trained to communicate in a specific style often prescribed by the trainer. Don't get me wrong—I think that process of controlled and specific communication style can be effective. Unfortunately, it can also create robots.

To be successful in certain jobs and roles in life requires specific personalities with specific communication styles. Nobody wants a technical or financial advisor to seldom provide a personal opinion. Their expertise is the reason we want them to be engaged in the process. Nor do we want the foreman of a construction crew to only give direction when it is comfortable and not personally threatening. This approach could come at the cost of serious construction errors. Or at least I don't want that construction crew building my house! Most, if not all of us, want to know it was accomplished with laser precision guided by a foreman who moved the crew along the process with a succinct plan and confidence.

With many life experiences guiding us, my wife and I had decisions to make. From the minute we started talking about our approach, there was one consistency we agreed upon. I was 100 percent committed to being open and honest about my disease. It was not clear as to the exact and specific pathway for doing so, but there was no doubt in my mind. I had seen too many friends and family only tell a handful of people of severe medical issues. Often, the healing powers of human compassion and community are lost in that situation. That path was not for me. On the flip side, I was not going to shout this out from the rooftop. Specifically, I knew I wanted to let those who were close to me be informed. Not knowing how my life might progress, disclosure seemed the best path.

We still needed to get through July 13th, just the second day of my diagnosis. The appointment with neurology was intended to provide the needed information to have a complete understanding of the exact severity of my disease, the prognosis, and the potential treatments. After much discussion, my wife and I decided the best path was to not tell anyone until after we had an opportunity to spend time with the doctor on July 13, the next day. But wait, our son, who was living out on his own at the time, and our daughter, who was home from college, were planning on a family dinner on July 12th at our house. We couldn't keep this from them this evening. Not fair. My wife and I formulated our message for the kids as we sat at lunch and were ready for the evening. After leaving the restaurant at lunch, I went back to my office. I had to respond to a few items and gather a few things to work from home the next day.

As my wife prepared pasta for us that evening, the kids arrived. We asked the kids to come to the kitchen as we had to talk with them. We told them of the diagnosis with the fact we knew very little at this point. It was affirmed to them; I was not imminently dying. My son stopped me and said, "Well that is not true, Dad. We are all slowly moving towards death in some way." Now that is perspective. My daughter's reaction was a joking reference to me trying marijuana to control the symptoms and needing to start "smoking weed." Twenty minutes later as we were eating, my two adult children sat at the table and jokingly flipped food at one another as part of a joke and argument. My wife and I looked at each other and said, "Either our children are incredibly resilient and well-adjusted in life, or they have mental health situations we need to address!" And this is not to diminish mental disorders, as my family are significant advocates for mental health awareness. Both my son and I have psychology degrees and my wife has a degree in sociology. My wife and I were simply amazed at their ability to process.

As my wife and I look back at this phase of our lives, we have since referred to the dinner with our children as the first stop on the "Disclosure Tour." As with any communication happening rapidly, there is often a pattern and process difficult to recognize and sometimes control. Luckily for us, we had formulated a plan in the first 48 hours and had control of the process. This reaction came from disseminating information and stories from the many great leaders I have had communication with and learned from prior. I would advise this approach to anyone going through such a situation. The disclosure tour had great similarity to other communication situations we have all experienced. We defined our audience for each portion of the tour, spending time understanding who in our circle of trust was needing proactive communication. There were those friends who would hear it secondhand, and we understood this would occur. Thus, it became essential to formulate a direct message proactively communicated in a succinct and specific cadence and process.

On July 13th, we visited with the doctor, read test results, looked at images, and came up with a short-term plan of attack. We were still trying to understand the depth and breadth of Parkinson's. We were confused and looking for information as quickly as we could find it. We knew a few key items. One million Americans have Parkinson's, 10 million across the globe. Ten percent of those are diagnosed with young onset before the age of 50. (The age of young onset is different among experts. It is sometimes quoted as 40, but most often it is 50 or higher.) My symptoms, when put together with the test results, are a certain diagnosis, As it now appears, I likely had been suffering from this for more than five years. My disease was in the early stages in many ways. In other ways, I had symptoms that would soon prove to be difficult to manage. No matter the symptoms and treatment, it was obviously Parkinson's Disease (PD). We left the doctor's office and went down the street to a quiet bar with a great outside patio. The previous hour had been very disturbing, confusing, and calming all at the same time.

Calming? Yes, calming. There was finally relief of the uncertainty and the beginning of a path. The path would hopefully provide a course of treatment and understanding. As the doctor said to me, "You knew something was not right, didn't you?" I could only nod my head in agreement, knowing this was not a proud moment.

To the medical professionals who told me I was just imagining an illness and symptoms, I hold no ill will. To those doctors who did not properly follow protocol, namely two of my team at that time, shame on you for not following an evidence-based medical and scientific approach. I know those two are an extremely small percentage of the tremendous doctors and nurses who wake up every day and pursue excellence in treating their communities. I can't say enough about the great medical staffs I have encountered.

As my wife, Deann, and I entered the patio area of the bar in downtown Des Moines, she saw a couple of folks she knew from her United Way world (Deann was the CEO of United Ways of Iowa). I needed to go to the restroom, and she went over to say hello to them. When I came out, it was clear to me she had told them. She said she hadn't, but their behavior told me other. I completely understood why she had. She needed to tell someone . . . anyone. We had a drink and then knew what was next. The disclosure tour was not just in rehearsal mode and completing warm-up gigs. We were live and launching.

We made a list of those who needed to be directly communicated with, dividing the list up into several segments. For a few of our groups, we would send a text with the message we did not want to inform them this way, but wanted them to know firsthand and would follow up soon with them. For others, we knew a direct phone call was in order.

The first calls were to my parents and mother-in-law. I have not ever had an official father-in-law. My wife's father passed of a sudden heart attack when she was a senior in high school. She is amazingly resilient in many ways for dealing with such a tough situation. That great trait and her many other skills were a part of her homelife and had already been passed on before her father's death. Her parents raised her with an almost identical set of values and beliefs as I was raised. Bird of a feather, or so the story goes.

Calling my parents was not easy. They took the phone call well. It could not be in person, as they live two hours away and I could not get over to their house that quickly. They knew this was a possibility. I knew my mother would want to know all the details I could share. That has always been her way, staying informed and aware. In fact, my brother and I often joked as we were growing up we needed to have standard documents and forms filled out in our house every time there was news. This included such items as new friends or girlfriends, one of our friends being in trouble or other changing dynamics in our worlds. I told her once she could have been an expert interrogator for the CIA, as she could get to the bottom of any situation with a set of questions designed to get a person to talk. She is not threatening in any way. She is just effective at getting the needed information. Remember, she was dealing with two boys (three if you count my father) that may not have been as thorough and forthcoming with details.

My father is always looking on the positive side of life. This is especially true immediately when he hears negative news. He did not grow up with a lot of wealth and was one of seven children with a wide gap in ages. This meant he and his younger sister learned to take care of themselves in many ways, as they were much younger than the others. My father often tells stories of irritating his sister just to get a good laugh from the planned incident. Sounds kind of mean until you see them today after all these years still giving each other a little razing. My father to this day laughs at my aunt throwing a toaster at him. Yes, a toaster. This is a little inside humor for my Cook family to enjoy (it is my first book, I need to sell copies, and they will buy anything their family is embedded within.)

My humorous father and my mother have led an amazing and successful life. They would communicate their life together has met most all their expectations of success in the world. They are inspirations to many, including our family. It is an amazing story best left for another book (keep buying my books, please.)

My mother-in-law, Pat, was eerily similar to my parents in her reaction to the news we communicated. My parents and Pat grew up in similar households with similar values. Pat understood the facts of our current medical situation as we knew them and was very supportive of my wife. Pat had lost a husband at the age of 40 and had lost a male companion (a spouse without the marriage) in 2016. She has been through a lot of grief and bad news. She is a survivor and was able to assist my wife in gaining perspective quickly.

Then, off we went on our disclosure tour to fill in gaps the rest of those friends and loved ones were starting to wonder about. For quite some time, I had been showing outward signs that concerned many around me. Of course, those closest to me sensed a pending conclusion or answer. We were somewhat matter of fact which typically was said as, "Troy has young on-set Parkinson's Disease (YOPD.)" The reactions were many. Shock, surprise, tears, hugs, and blank stares.

Our neurologist told us to be prepared for the obligatory response often accompanying YOPD news. The response goes something like this: "OH! (gasp) . . . you have PD (pause for a blank stare from the person to me or my wife) . . . I am sorry." We were told my wife would get this most often. Spot on with that advice. Often, I would watch as we would casually mention this to a friend or two and they would look at me first, then look at my wife with the "Oh, your husband has PD" face. It is a normal human reaction. Most have little knowledge of how a 48-year-old, other than Michael J. Fox, could have this thing called PD. The questions and images they formed were understandable. I had the same reaction when I was told (see chapter 3). If chapter 3 is read again at this point, it will lengthen the time it takes to read this book, thus increasing the value of the purchase.

Communicating the correct information in the correct order became clear to us. We are blessed with great groups of friends tied to many different aspects of our lives. One such large group of friends comes from our kids' Catholic education community. This is a group of adults and children who take community engagement seriously. When they need to mobilize and act, get involved or get the heck out of the way, they will get it done. We have been involved in delivering meals to those who are ill to providing car rides for children of those going through cancer treatment (thanks to two of our friends willing to let us help…we will always be grateful to be a part of their lives). We are thankful for this type of response. Knowing the facts of young onset Parkinson's as we knew them, we often began in telling this group I was not disabled, not going to be disabled soon, and not imminently dying. PD patients can live long healthy lives. Understanding these facts helps lessen the fear and shock of the news. Just ask our children, as they threw food at each other when they found out.

We knew the communications would allow us to receive the prayers of a community, but not the casseroles from a chain of families. The last thing I needed was to gain more weight! Almost immediately, there was a group asking to bring us food. My response was maybe a bit harsh; "For 20 years? They are bringing us meals for 20 years?" I was a little over-reactive to help and assistance at this point. Our friends are amazing people and were trying to help. I was just a little over reactive and sensitive to accepting the diagnosis. At least this is the rationale a therapist provided to me. As the therapist said, "Calm down and appreciate those who want to assist and comfort you AND YOUR FAMILY." Yes, those are all caps words as she yelled at me in her own special way. I am not sure, but believe she was a little taken back at my attitude. Well observed and communicated by her. Maybe she should be writing a book.

With any communication plan, there are always surprises. As I mentioned earlier, having a specific and succinct message is key. Surprises, in hindsight, are recognizable. In our situation, they came in two distinct forms. The first was overreaction and exaggerated stories. The second were the negative and upsetting reactions.

According to one storyline we heard circulating, my wife and I were picking out long-term care facilities for me to be a part of within about 90 days of us sharing the news of PD. While it is true that we did share our news with several people, we did not place the news on social media. We did ask those we talked with to correct any misinformation they might of heard and refrain from spreading any uncertain speculation. We told many of our friends, "Just ask me what you want to know." After all, I have a bachelor's degree in psychology, did some clinical practicums in counseling, completed rat research on conditioned responses, and have pretended to be an expert to thousands and thousands of folks I have presented to. Surely, I am an expert.

Many people asked me questions. Being informed as a communicator is really important. It helps sharpen communication, as those who are uninformed typically need succinct education. This is true across all of life. We all like to spout off our own opinions. I am great at it. My opinions really matter and are often the correct ones (that is a joke, by the way. I mention the jokes in this book once again for those who are not catching the odd, but funny, sense of humor.) In the case of massive change or life-altering events, having expertise is important to providing comfort and confidence to the message. Remember, each audience is unique, but all audiences want knowledge, information, expertise, and wisdom. More on wisdom later in this book.

My daughter also was asked by one of her friends how she was dealing with my pending death, in a roundabout line of questioning. At one point during the early months of the disclosure tour, I apparently had a form of neurological disease known as ALS. This is not comical, as ALS is a horrific neurological disease. One of my friends passed away from ALS just as I was getting diagnosed with PD. Jim was a great man. Knowing this, I understand the comparisons. But as Jim's wife told my wife, "Come on, people, know your diseases before you react." I wish all who read this book to please pause for a short moment to remember anyone who may have a friend or loved one pass of ALS.

This is a good life lesson on communication. We may have researched and prepared for each of the audiences to be confronted, but it is always difficult and complex to predict the outcome. This is why we must be ready to adapt to the situation as it evolves. This does not mean sticking to the current communication plan and audiences as planned. Situations and those people involved in those situations evolve. Change is inevitable. As a result, these evolutions; whether friends, customers, or workplace teammates, self-selection occurs. The people on any one team change. This should not be news to anyone, but it is often tough to read and accept.

Self-selection is messy, difficult and confusing. Self-selection is not always conscious. We stop communicating with a friend or group of friends because of a lack of commonality. It may be a situation that caused us to be upset, or just a growing apart.

Businesses see this manifest in annual turnover. When employees are not onboard with the mission of a company, it becomes easy for staff to move to another employer. A fifty cent an hour pay increase may make enough difference for a colleague to find themselves in a more suitable workplace. There are employers who know they will have high turnover due to the nature of their work. It does not mean they should just give up on trying to communicate the effectiveness and importance of each team member, but we often see this. Their lack of communication then becomes a lack of knowledge and information in the workplace. When we have a lack of information, unfortunately, we often believe in the worst-case scenario and prepare ourselves accordingly. It is a human reaction for survival.

Don't confuse this lack of information and poor communication with being resilient to a changing environment. If we have basic information and knowledge, we make effective decisions promoting our own resiliency. Without information, we prepare for the worst in some way, albeit a small manner. This allows each of us to begin the process of protecting ourselves for survival. Survival instincts are a basic human reaction. Without them, we would not have made it far enough to read this book. Many reference the common "fight or flight" reactions we have in life.

Believe it or not, I have lost friends due to my diagnosis. This falls into the second category of negative reactions. Just like the employee not feeling "bought into" the company they work for, we all have friends not "bought into" our friendship. This does not make them bad people. We can't be friends with everybody. We are all unique and don't get along with everyone.

If this is unpleasant news, I am sorry. All should feel free to shut this book now and go find something else to do. Life is full of choices. Living in reality is one of them. Those who chose to not live in reality, can find a new outlet for their time at this point of the book. Why face reality now? The rest of the information I am sharing in this book will not be in agreement with those wishing to bury their heads in the sand. Hoping with no specific plan is not usually the best approach. It may appear to be a brighter, more enlightened choice, but the light may be a steaming locomotive train at the end of the tunnel. It is not likely to find the brakes before crashing into every object or barrier in its way. But if it is easier to just ignore reality, stopping here in the reading is great. Let us all group hug and sing a lovely parting tune. However, we all know when faced with unpleasant news, life does go on. Darn it, as this was not the promised perfect world. How dare I call out the "don't disrupt my utopia with reality" crowd.

Just because we can't be friends with everyone does not mean we can't be nice to all we meet and respect those who earn and maintain our respect. The most successful companies in the world understand not everyone will buy their product. Even conglomerates such as Microsoft and Facebook don't have 100 percent market share. Yet that does not stop us from trying to attain 100 percent market share or being genuine and respectful to 100 percent of those we meet. But sometimes, there is no relationship to be developed. We all must accept this as fact and move on, grow up, get over it. Each of us in the world must focus on what can be controlled.

This reminds me of a man I have had the pleasure of talking to in detail several times; I will call him Randy (not his real name). He is from a small rural community about two hours from a major metro area in the U.S. He had built a successful insurance agency from scratch. He has represented his industry on national boards and commissions and been honored countless times for his volunteer and professional work. I asked him once why he had not sold his practice to a larger firm providing him with resources to expand. This would potentially grow his practice into the suburbs of the metro area he was close to. He looked back over his shoulder at me as we walked and smiled. Then he laughed and explained he had loyalty to his community. He knew not everyone wants to do business the way he does. Many of his clients are personal friends. If he was part of a different firm, he would lose those personal connections. He knew and understood his audience in detail. They liked his message, and he liked being a part of their lives. His communication was and is still excellent. He knows his audience, has embraced his calling in life, has and will continue communicating with a specific plan and intent. He has been and will be excellent at his job and the communication needed to be successful. End of story.

FIVE

─────❧─────

Ctrl+Alt+Del

Most everyone has had the difficult and frustrating moment in life when a computer malfunctions. It freezes, makes an awkward noise, closes programs automatically, or any other number of strange and bizarre situations. For those who may be reading this book and are IT or help desk specialists, this computer malfunction situation does not usually draw much concern. For others, this causes extreme stress, concerns, and use of multiple four-letter words in strange sequence. And by the way, when I was growing up, who knew there would be a job in a department called "Help Desk"?

Like most of us, I am not equipped to solve complicated computer issues. Many of us are blessed to work with tremendously resourceful individuals who are more than equipped to handle complicated computer issues. I do know the basics to get me out of a jam with frozen screens and other simple issues.

Which reminds me of another one of my stories that drags on endlessly, according to my family. By the way, this is when my wife will look at me and say, "Yes, make the story move along please."

For a number of days, I had been going through quite a few issues with my laptop computer. I was traveling a lot and spending a great deal of time on the phone with "experts" attempting to work through the computer issues. We were successful in getting me only limited access for the two days I needed until I was back in the office. Then, one of the experts could have my laptop in front of them to work on it solving each of the complex problems it presented by merely turning it on and off again. Seeing an opportunity for humor, I took an old obsolete computer from home and smashed a little of it up and tore out a few other pieces. Putting the pieces in a clear bag, I placed the bag on my desk when I arrived back in the office. Subsequently, calling the help desk resource I was working with, informing them my laptop was on my desk waiting for their expert skills, the trap had been set. After the tech arrived, he saw the pile of parts. I informed him that I kicked the computer, as I had seen that work with a desktop version of the same brand prior. His shock was nothing short of amazing. No smile, no frown, no words, just a blank stare at the bag of parts. After what seemed to be a long period, I quickly pulled out my laptop and let him in on the joke. He did not think the joke was funny. He merely explained to me how the kicking and dropping of computers only makes his life more difficult. Well intentioned on my part. Not well taken on his. My officemates around me all thought it was hysterical! Many who read this story will relate and laugh as well.

As with all of my stories, there is a lesson. Earlier, we briefly explored and applied the concept of "Ctrl+ALt+Del". In doing so, we addressed the "task manager" we are faced with when taking time to hit reset. That concept and it's applications deserve a deeper dive, so here it is. The recently told pile of computer parts story in the previous paragraphs is a great example of reseeting to begin our extended discussion on Ctrl+Alt+Del.

Just as with a computer, when life seems to be locked up or a problem does not seem to be moving towards resolution, "kicking" with no real intent does not work. It may feel good to kick the can down the road or express raw anger, but it usually ends up in a bag of parts needing to be put back together again. As with all good advice from any computer expert (and assuming we are using Windows), it is best to hit the keys Ctrl+Alt+Del at the same time. This accomplishes a step back and assessment of the entire situation before resorting to the standard dropkick. It is an amazing metaphor for life. When faced with a change that appears too unfamiliar, unwieldy, or causes severe hesitation in moving forward, resetting the view of the situation is a great next step.

If there is such a person who has not ever been to a point in life with change and problems starting to become difficult to manage, there is a likely lack of awareness of the world around them. People and businesses run into this constantly. Recognizing there is change is vital, communicating the change to others is crucial, and managing the situation going forward requires Ctrl+Alt+Del.

As a quick reminder, when we hit Ctrl+Alt+Del on a computer, we are faced with choices. They include shutting down the computer, restarting the computer, logging off, or assessing our task manager. For obvious reasons, the analogies of shutting down and logging off are a little more complicated to explain in a metaphor for life. Not sure we have a choice of just shutting down or logging off. That is not an option suggested or advocated for by anyone. However, most often, the choice we make on the computer is the task manager. This makes sense, as we can see programs running well, programs not running or responding, programs we did not know were open, the programs running we had no idea were even on our computer, or a virus or rogue program attempting to cause intentional harm.

Hitting Ctrl+Alt+Del in our personal and work lives has a similar value to doing this on the computer. Assessing one's personal task manager is often enlightening. Based upon my conversations with those whom have tremendous success and fulfillment in life, this enlightened assessment is a worthwhile process. I have had this believe affirmed during my battle with Parkinson's. Often, I have found myself assessing the pathways of life to better understand if each is accomplishing a goal. Or possibly the pathway or process is not progressing as I thought, or is causing a distraction towards other goals. Of course, there are occasionally those around us personally or within our companies who serve as inhibitors to the progress needed to accomplish goals. Unfortunately, there are also those who intentionally cause the pathways to success to jam up.

Just three weeks after being diagnosed with Parkinson's, and in the middle of trying to communicate to those we thought appropriate, my wife and I took a long, overdue trip from Iowa (where we live) to Colorado. It is about a 10-hour drive. Perfect time to hit Ctrl+Alt+Del and assess. Our plans included a few days in Denver to see a concert with one of my lifelong friends. Afterwards, we would then head up to the mountains to do nothing specific for five more nights. To me, this is a near perfect vacation. A time to rest and recover with little preplanned activity or the requirement of deep thought.

While on our long drive, we started to take inventory of the facts as we knew them at that time regarding our enormously changing life together. One such revelation was quick and easy to assess within days of my diagnosis. It was the likelihood I would not live much beyond the age of 70. Based upon my set of symptoms, the outcomes of those symptoms, and other factors, my pathway was likely not to live a long and healthy retirement. It is just a fact. It could turn out differently, and planning on a different outcome may sound optimistic, but could be foolish. Of course, I am working towards having a long and healthy retirement. However, planning for a shorter alternative is smart and thoughtful to those around me. This means making sure we are in a good spot financially. We had to gain an understanding of the decisions needing to be addressed as the disease progresses. This would also include having meaningful and frank conversations with those who will be a part of the change.

The recognition of my future life was an almost automatic and instinctive reaction. I'm not sure why. For my wife, understanding the situation was more difficult. For most people who are not the victim of such a disease, the process of assessing the facts is often more difficult. Maybe it is the brain playing tricks on each of us, but there is a definite difference. Without having hit Ctrl+Alt+Del, this recognition and realization would have been much more difficult to assess.

It has been a great privilege to have talked with many who have faced a diagnosis of Parkinson's, cancer, MS, or other life-altering and life-threatening medical issues. There are a few amazing observations in the difference in attitude those patients of treatable but life-threatening diseases have compared to those with progressive diseases. Many times, we hear people diagnosed with cancer vow "to beat this." It is always humbling to observe the courage and persistence of those who fight and attack such a diagnosis. When talking to those with the diagnosis, they will often relay the innate ability to fight against the cancer or other diagnosis. Our minds take over for the body. When the disease is pushed back, cancer patients will often convey the fear of relapse or finding a new concern related to the previous cancer. In almost every aspect of their lives, the never-ending fear can have significant impact.

When visiting with those who have a progressive disease, such as Parkinson's, there is an inner acceptance with their diagnosis. My theory is the human mind and body is hitting Ctrl+Alt+Del and assessing the facts of the situation. Once acceptance occurs, the next steps are influenced by several factors. Those include age of diagnosis, other medical conditions present, long-term prognosis and many other disease specific factors. For those with young-onset Parkinson's, such as myself, the reaction witnessed in my observations tend to fall into two categories. The first is acceptance and subsequently getting on a path forward, fighting as hard as possible to stop the progression in the most effective manner possible.

The other reaction is not like the first in almost any way. It is summarized as giving up, accepting fate, and watching the body fall apart. My strong belief is most start with an assessment of their life task manager. However, those who just give up trying to fight had not completed the full process of evaluating their "task manager." They often will accept a rapid decline of their body and mind. It is often not their own fault or lack of ability. Unfortunately, we all have innate preset mechanisms to deal with life changes. Those mechanisms may need to be altered to accept, assess, and move forward from hearing "you have a life-altering, progressive, neurological disease with no known cure."

It is not uncommon for a comparison of the process of acceptance of diagnosis to be compared to the grieving process. There is a loss of the life and goals one had imagined. Grieving experts say there is often a process our mind goes through when diagnosed with such a disease or incurable medical condition. It does truly imitate the process of grieving the loss of life. Part of the process is often anger and finally acceptance. This is true of many with whom I have talked with after having their own life altering diagnosis. However, there is a major difference between grieving the loss of a loved one and being diagnosed with Parkinson's at age 48. The ongoing disease is present and causing living hell with the body while there is still a processing of the magnitude of the situation. Ctrl+Alt+Del becomes extremely important for the remainder of life.

Businesses have similar issues with accepting the diagnosis of a negative change or unforeseen results. When a product is no longer cutting edge or becomes too expensive for consumers, companies must often react quickly. Acceptance of the changing world is difficult. We see companies refuse to understand the change. They often never open the task manager to understand the situation with which they are dealing. They don't recognize there is inevitable change.

We all know the names of such companies. Kodak, Blockbuster—insert many big retailer names here. All had great products they offered and market share. The world keeps changing and new information is presented to consumers constantly. This happens to small, medium, and large businesses alike. It is nondiscriminatory. It is the nature of business. Most all of these companies have not or had not bothered to hit

Ctrl+Alt+Del. Doing so could have allowed assessment of the changing world in which they were living. Most of these organizations likely had tried to reassess but were often stuck in the grieving process phase of not accepting the facts as they were.

We all see companies try "new ideas," which are really the same core strategies with slightly new process to them. They do not address the need to change the goals. Mission and vision can still be creditable and core, but goals may adapt to the current environment. Trying to reinvent strategies to accommodate the same outdated goals does not create an opportunity for growth. It only moves or adjusts the chairs on the deck of the Titanic. The boat still sinks. If we remember the mission is to safely navigate the waters to deliver the passengers to their destination, this becomes much clearer. If the goal is to put luxury and the lack of disruption of such luxury ahead of the mission, then the mission becomes compromised. All strategies going forward are irrelevant. Unfortunately, we know the ending to this story. The boat still sinks every time I watch Titantic.

For years, we have seen companies take employees and leaders on "planning retreats" and "strategic planning sessions." All are great and needed. I have been on these. They can be great in many ways. They can also be a waste of valuable human and financial resources. In the first months of my Parkinson's diagnosis, I learned a great deal of how to assess a needed change in strategy or goals. Don't get the wrong impression. My learning was not because I made perfect assessments and decisions. In many situations, just the opposite. There were a few "ah-ha" moments. One such occurred during our trip to Colorado. Neither the readers nor the editor of this book thought I would ever arrive back at this story. In fact, one proofer made a rather snide comment about my jumping back to the Colorado story. So, in that proofer's honor, the Colorado trip was with my wife just a few weeks after being diagnosed with PD.

Deann and I have seldom been on the same clock cycles in our marriage. Typically, I have always been an earlier riser than my wife. I envy her ability to sleep and relax in the mornings. I also envy her ability to stay up late and still be productive the next morning. While in the mountains of Colorado, we stayed at a condo in Keystone. Great place to stay. Excellent place to hit Ctrl+Alt+Del. Getting up early by myself most mornings in the mountains is very therapeutic.

During this trip, it was a reminder to me there are only a few folks out early, but it is quiet and peaceful. I would fix breakfast and sit outside, staring at the mountains. I made lists . . . lots of lists. They included questions about my disease, aspects of my financial world I would need to check out, ideas of how to adjust my lifestyle, and countless other lists. Many were not relevant to anything other than the process of sorting through the multiple task manager programs running in my life. This helped me to define which parts or processes of my life were running properly, not running well, or not even needed in order to move forward. As I reviewed these lists and thoughts, it seemed overwhelming at least a few moments of every day. After all, I was only three weeks out from my diagnosis.

This is not dissimilar to the many great organizations I have worked with over the years. The acceptance of change, reviewing the task manager of goals and strategies, and moving forward is a massive undertaking. Again, a little bit like the grieving process. Each step needs to be completed to properly make wise decisions about the future.

On one of my first days in the mountains, I had a moment

of great influence on my life going forward. Now, a little background is important. The fresh mountain air is amazing, especially in the morning. Being up at 9,000 feet has an impact on the brain. Oxygen is thinner, all of us move a little slower, and have to drink lots of water adjusting to the environmental conditions. Often, folks who visit the fresh mountain air describe these similar feelings. Inherently, due to this heightened state of awareness of one's body, the thought process on life is different as well.

After breakfast one morning, I took my computer and a notepad down to an area where there were several folks participating in mountain-type activities, from renting bikes to buying turns on a giant swing-type device with a trampoline and lots of safety equipment. There were parents trying to convince kids they should not spend money on these items, and grandparents asking kids what they wanted to do next, spending any amount of money to satisfy the grandchildren. It is the great divide between being a parent and grandparent. I was sitting under an umbrella at a table with the Rocky Mountains on all sides in 65-degree sunshine. There was little to no humidity, and a lack of oxygen.

Without knowing it, my life change was beginning to move to the stage of acceptance. Assessing the areas of my world I could have an impact on, I realized my goals in life had been adjusted. It was an amazing and completely humbling experience. Yet, a calming moment. We have all had this experience. It is the moment the current task manager of life has been accepted. I could no longer think about the goals of the past, but had to focus on the needs of the current situation to impact the future. It was the beginning of discovering my current identity and the future envisioned.

Was there a sudden life-changing moment in a few seconds sitting at that picnic table? No. Did I start to see my surroundings subconsciously as I was consciously writing and thinking about my goals in life? Yes. Over the course of an hour or two, I had started to form adjusted and new goals. Key word being *adjusted*. Yes, there were new goals. But the current goals did not require complete abandonment. Just like our computer analogy, not all programs and functions have to be stripped from the computer. There were aspects that needed to be altered, but complete abandonment is not a requirement for any individual or organization when evaluating the factors of change and growth.

Keep in mind, there had been attempts to physically cope with this unknown world prior to my diagnosis. The new medicines were already starting to take effect. Exercise and limited pain relief were now a part of most days. Far from perfect, but I was moving forward while making my adjustments. My core principles and beliefs in life remained intact.

My pathways to affect the mission and vision had changed. An interesting question comes to mind. Wasn't the path of life always going to be filled with change anyway? Yes! Remember, change is inevitable. All of us will have to adjust to the change of life, no matter the change. Despite being superhuman as I am, my situation was no different. And I am superhuman; 5'11, bald, not totally lean at this point in my life, possessing an awkward walking style, and over-confident. The definition of superhuman should have a picture of me next to it. We can't stop most change happening within our world. Nobody can have the same life tomorrow as today. Failure to recognize this will only cause pain and suffering both in the short- and long-term aspects of an organization and each of our lives.

Often, when companies try to embark on the process of adjusting their goals, they forget to accept the fact just described; there was always going to be needed adjustment. The acceptance of staying status quo is not and was not an option. Because the world is changing, the factors impacting success and failure each day are different.

Many of us have been asked the question by a leader or asked it ourselves, "Why should we change?" or "What is the case for change." They may seem like good question, but one could argue to alter the question slightly: "What is the change in the world around us, and how can we find opportunities for growth?" Of course, this does not mean changing the mission and vision. It may not mean altering any of the goals. However, at minimum it will likely mean the strategies to affect the mission will have to change. Goals may be altered, and metrics reassessed, but mission and vision are likely still in place. This assumption is based upon the mission and vision being broad enough for long term relevance. All missions and visions should be this broad. However, there are mistakes made and they become too specific.

If facts indicate the mission and vision of a company are no longer relevant, then serious questions must be asked. Was the mission too specific or the vision overly exact? Often there is confusion on the definition of mission and vision. This usually results with missions that are really goals. In organizational research and many shared experiences, we can observe successful mission and vision statements are broad-based, and not specific goals. Specific goals will be sought after to affect the mission and vision. We have all read mission statements which are really stating one or several goals. Those examples have great intention, but the wrong execution. Most highly successful companies and individuals will communicate this same experience. They have had missteps with confusion on goals, mission and vision.

As individuals, we have most likely seen the same. It can become all too easy to chase goals not connecting with our core vision of life. Even more problematic is allowing society to define our mission instead of our own specific and intentional definition.

In keeping with our computer analogy, as we all review our task manager in resetting the current world, we are not asking to change the fundamental mission of the computer. The mission of owning a computer is to provide an effective and efficient means of electronic medium for multiple purposes. One goal underneath the mission may be to have word processing at the fingertips of the user. The strategy for such a goal is to load and run a word-processing program. How effective the word-processing program of choice is, can be measured and results can be assessed. If a user never plans on using the computer for word processing, then why have a word-processing program. Stop spending time on it. Move on!

It all sounds so easy as typed and in this chapter. Set goals, measure, reassess, measure, etc. However, life is not always so simple. Business is not always so simple. Change happens all around us. Good news, bad news, natural disasters, human disasters, being diagnosed with Parkinson's. It all happens. Being able to hit Ctrl+Alt+Del can fundamentally alter the view of the change and allow for a more successful path forward. It is seldom heard anywhere in the world, "We were too aware of all the facts, processes and factors influencing our current situation, causing us to make overly informed and wise decisions. And this lead to our demise."

SIX

———❦———

There Is "ME" in Team

How often do we hear the intended to be inspirational words, "There is no 'I' in team." Often enough it has become a tongue in cheek comment in situations. It occasionally is taken too far and becomes a rant instead of inspirational.

While the no "I" statement is true, it should be noted there is an "M" and "E," which spells "Me"!

Please don't think I am not a team player. I am. I coached football at the high school level, did a stint early in my career with college coaching. Even coached my son in middle school football. Was a track coach and worked with numerous athletes over the years in my speaking and consulting. Team is an important concept to me.

We hear leaders from all walks of business, industry, athletics, theatre, etc. pontificate about team. Most have used the "no 'I' in team" line at some point in their careers. No denying how important a team is to the world around us. The metaphor of a chain and its weakest link is also referenced countless times by leaders looking to inspire and drive success. Hence, the concept of team becomes even more important. The team lifts each of us up to new heights as we work together. All true, all good, all inspiring. Never forget this paragraph as most would agree it is factual, not just opinion.

However, the very essence in much of the discussion of team revolves around having each member of a team identify, comprehend, and implement personal goals leading to greater team success. The most desired situation is for individual goals to align with team goals. However, it is often forgotten each of us is a unique human. We have our own DNA, experiences, and personality which forms our current and future self. Obvious from this observation is we all identify with a different set of goals. When success is defined on the basis of another's goals and aspirations, it becomes difficult for an individual or team to ever reach fulfillment. We discussed this concept extensively, earlier in this book.

Building a successful team is no different. If each member of the team has not clearly identified their own goals, the team goals often become a short-term fix for the lack of individual goals. This may work for an athletic season or the production of a play or movie. Actors and players can move in an out of roles and positions for a short period of time. But once the team goal is met there is often little or no connection between the members. Next, the team disbands, and the players and actors move on. Keeping the team together for a long period of time in a successful manner requires the "ME" in team. Without it, our individual efforts become meaningless as the focus is only on the team. Successful teams with longevity have

"Me" and "Team."

In any strong organizational structure, individuals each must accept their defined role. Team members must make adaptations for the good of the team. However, if we go too far away from our own definition of success, our work for the team becomes irrelevant. This sounds selfish, but upon closer examination it is an imperative concept to embrace in achieving success in each of our lives. There is evidence all around us. We change jobs, we make new friends, we stop hanging out with old friends. We form teams constantly in this world. And those teams constantly change. Just as each of us must accept and adapt to change, so do each of the teams we are a part of in life. It is a fundamental principle in life.

My journey of discovery with Parkinson's has been a driving force in recognizing the value of this principle. Defining the terms of success for each of us is crucial before we can ever identify the teams we want to be a part of. I learned a lot about my teams during the early days of my diagnosis. As well, the learnings also extended to awareness of how and why I was defining success in my own life. As one can imagine, the definition of success for me during those early months of fighting this disease was challenged and sometimes altered.

Despite having adverse conditions in our lives, most individuals still wake up and want to positively impact the lives of those around them. This could be defined as a belief in the human mission of all to be genuinely positive if given the opportunity and environment to do so. Inherently, almost all people want to live in a world where we provide meaningful value to those around us. For some, this is manifested in leadership roles and strategic directives. For others, it is part of a ministry of service to others and tactical in nature.

No matter the role, ultimately, we all want to show value in a measurable manner. It makes us feel good. I once had a company CEO tell me, "We all want to win. Either we compete with ourselves or against others constantly, but we all want to experience the feelings of winning." She further explained winning is a positive feeling. In her experience, the more she could create the positive feeling of winning within the culture of her company, the more successful her company became. She did not overtly state this in her goal setting and team meetings. Her fundamental actions as a leader were embedded in helping her team members "win, making each of us go home at night with positive attitudes."

Even in times of adversity, we want to provide value towards those we interact with, including ourselves. While it is impossible to be pulling and pushing at the same time, we want to find where we can fit best. Occasionally, we must accept help in trying to pull or push our way to success. And almost always, we need a team. No matter the form of the team, teams assist in reaching higher levels of success. Case in point: without multiple doctors, I would not have been able to discover and treat my diagnosis.

My primary care provider properly assessed the need for a consult with neurology. He did not really believe I was suffering from anything other than stress and hypochondriac behavior. When the first neurologist treated me with little compassion and skill in assessing my needs, his role on my team became diminished. His goals did not align with the rest of my small team, which only consisted of my wife and I at that time. He was not worried about a true diagnosis, but rather moving me through his world. He did not get the idea of "team." Then back to my primary care provider.

The second go-round with my primary care doctor was slightly better as he could see I was not content we were on the right path. There was little improvement and many of my symptoms were worsening. After blood tests and more inquiries, it became clear I was having issues. This likely came as a surprise to him, as he still believed it was not a serious situation. He referred me to rheumatology. My team was now growing, and it appeared the members were starting to get on board with unified goals and a future vision of diagnosis and treatment. My primary care doctor had finally figured out his role on my team, or so I thought at the time.

The rheumatologist served as a new team member who clearly understood his role. He treated the symptoms for a few months. However, at my insistence, I expressed concern over the lack of progress. To his credit, he referred me to a movement disorder specialist. My team grew by one more. All of us were in alignment on putting the pieces of this complex puzzle together. Each team member also had similarly aligned individual goals of assisting patients to pathways of improvement. Well, that may not be totally true as I would come to understand. At the time, however, it felt like an aligned team.

After my diagnosis, the team continued to change. The role of the rheumatologist was significantly lessened. My primary care doctor was less than compassionate about my diagnosis. He and his direct staff treated me as if I was making up my diagnosis when I had to interact with them shortly after. They had either not read or never received the file notes from Dr. Smith, the neurologist, with the diagnosis. In pointing this out to them, they then read the reports. Once they did see the complete diagnosis and follow up I was undertaking, there was no apology for their actions. It went even further with no recognition of the seriousness of my diagnosis. Other physicians have told me that this primary care doctor was most likely suffering from guilt. He had not recognized the symptoms nor taken me seriously with my initial concerns. He had let the process of diagnosis take at least 18 months. This embarrassment or guilt makes sense to me. It is now clear there were symptoms and indicators of Parkinson's four or more years prior to my diagnosis. If this is why he felt guilty, I understand and appreciate his feelings. However, the decision had to be made that he would no longer be a part of my team. The evolution of the team continued.

We all go through this process in our own personal and work lives with consistency. It can happen unintentionally and often without warning. It can also happen as a form of self-selection by others who do not want or chose to be a part of our world. Rather intentionally or not, we develop deep and specific relationships. These relationships have a meaningful purpose and outcome. If these outcomes don't align with our desired results, the relationship is altered going forward.

As mentioned, the team changed, as needed. On a long-term basis, individuals on the team can't find success individually or as a team unless all team members understand "me" first. Without this understanding of individual alignment to the team, individual team members are merely asking the team to just keep pulling and pushing in a direction with no idea as to why, how, and when.

Let me give you an easy-to-understand example.

Once my diagnosis was handed down to me, it became clear there were several medically necessary steps needing to be initiated. First, medicines were to be adjusted. A rheumatology follow-up was needed. His previously prescribed medications needed to be altered based upon new facts and goals of treatment. This required a consultation with him to define a plan of attack. One of my meds had a serious side effect when coming off the drug. As luck would have it, I experienced a great deal of the side effects. It was a difficult period for two months. Headaches, head zaps (like lightning bolts going off in my brain), and a few other minor symptoms. Once we completed the process of adjusting the rheumatology related prescriptions and treatment, my team changed. That specific doctor was no longer an integral part of the team. Also, his personal goals of treatment for rheumatological illness were not in alignment with the team goals. It is not a statement on his value as a physician or person. It was not right or wrong. It was now a different situation. It was sad to say, but he was becoming an irrelevant team member. Just like any other team in life, when there is no longer alignment, we move on.

My team changed to new personnel, each carrying a different set of personal and professional goals and expertise. Collectively, the goals were to allow me to live my best life. Before each of us could impact the other, we had to all identify and comprehend the individual success we were desiring. Those goals allowed for greater success for each of us.

As I have experienced, almost all but a few medical providers want to be a part of a patient's care team when they believe they can impact the person in a positive manner. They are trained to be "caregivers." It becomes their mission and vision in life to provide care. Their goals become centered around outcomes, patient experience, and impact on their patient's long-term success. Of course, like every career and industry, there are always a small number of providers who are more centered on their own misaligned mission than with the rest of the medical field. Those providers of care rarely find themselves a part of successful teams, especially the patient teams whom they could impact. Please don't judge the entire medical field on those very few exceptions.

My approach to building the team may sound a bit odd at first. After all, I was the one suffering. How could I think those now a part of the team needed to have their own goals before they could impact me? Should I not have been grounded in survival mode? These were all questions crossing my mind and asked of me by others whom I shared my journey with.

At first, thinking in survival mode was my approach. My experience in life of discovering and telling stories of success from others should have alerted me to the many approaches to consider in this situation. Unfortunately, life is just not that simple. Although there was the "ah-ha" moment on vacation in Colorado described earlier, there was still the initial shock that had not completely dissipated The shock was both mentally and physically impactful. Luckily, thanks to the many examples from others over the years, our team evolved to meet the current needs. This was a jump out of survival mode and into continued recognition of finding pathways to grow.

My neurologist laid out a plan of managing the physical symptoms, as we knew them, at the time of diagnosis. Unfortunately for her, she did not see many young-onset patients. She had a few, but her expertise was in treating those who were at a more advanced age. However, she was engaged in research. This was important to me, although not because I was a candidate for her research. Knowing she was inquisitive and looking for a deeper sense of the cause of Parkinson's indicated her dedication to patients. This was and continues to be important to me. My goals with this disease were to not go down without one hell of a massive, all punches thrown, exhausting bruising fight like no other in history. The decision was made to fight harder than I could even imagine. A neurologist who was performing research clearly had a similar goal in her professional career. As recognized in hindsight, this was the beginning of adjustment and adaptation to goals.

The new team was being formed with an adjusted definition of success. The team now needed to be aligned with the goal of "impacting others through my journey." Looking back, there was not a clear appreciation for the complete impact this goal could have. It was not completely possible to grasp the potential impact, as the journey was still so fresh and new. Hence the need for all of us to have a team around us that is aligned with our defined goals. Each team member brings their own aligned goals and perspectives accepting their roles, and executing strategy as best they can. At least this is the formula for most of the successful teams that have been built.

Earlier, I talked about Coach M and his amazing ability to communicate with his players and their parents. He also provides numerous examples of understanding the "me" defined in team. I asked him once about his decision to stay in his role as head football coach in his hometown. Clearly, he had been approached to pursue opportunities outside of his current role. And likely at least a few of these roles would have advanced his financial picture as well as given him the opportunity to implement his strong core belief system in life.

He mentioned to me two unique stories. One was a personal story of his career path. The other, a football story occurring with just one of his players. Personal story first.

Coach M had been approached regarding numerous opportunities to pursue careers outside of teaching and coaching throughout his tenure. When he started sharing this story, I thought I could clearly see the direction we were going. I assumed he almost took a job as a financial planner or insurance agent he mentioned receiving, serving his local community. He could still serve as a beacon of guidance for all of those he served throughout his teaching and coaching career. Wrong answer.

Although he had received such offers, his decision to move to become an administrator was the one of most significant points of his career, according to him. He had seen turnover in the leadership above him at the school; he felt run down and stagnant, and knew he wanted to be challenged further. Amazingly enough, he discovered this desired challenge directly in front of him. An opening to become activities director. His team alignment would change slightly, but he could easily identify a path to accomplishing his personal goals while maintaining the journey of his coaching career. Of course, his salary changed slightly. He only mentioned salary after I asked him about it. He had defined who he was based upon his role in the team. Compensation was a secondary goal. He believed compensation would take care of itself. Amazingly enough, he mentioned to me the experience of becoming activities director was a reset to his life! Ctrl+Alt+Del. This was back in the 1980s, so the concept of Ctrl+Alt+Del would have been a foreign concept! However, reset was not a unfamiliar word. He hit reset and moved forward.

The other story of having firm individual convictions in order to be a strong team he conveyed occurred in the middle of a football season. He had a young but talented quarterback, who we will call Adam. Adam was playing as the younger backup to a highly successful senior leader. The senior was a beacon of leadership in Coach M's system: intensely competitive, confident, but relaxed and carried himself with dignity. Adam had a great deal to learn by watching his older teammates. Adam was two years younger and saw his career as a two-year starter beginning the following year. His time playing on the Junior Varsity (JV) team would be a chance to show off his ability, have some fun, and improve his personal talent. At least those were his views according to Coach. Coach had another view.

During one of the first several JV games Adam was playing in as a sophomore, Coach was on the sidelines as more of a spectator and not a coach. He did this often during JV and middle school football so other coaches could have the opportunity to coach in a leadership role. This also allowed him to maintain the mystique around making it to the varsity level. Coach was always involved in supporting every level of his programs, just not the decision maker during JV games. The players knew this as well. If Coach did visit with one of them on the sidelines, it was often a moment of teaching and instruction. Adam was very much aware of Coach's presence and role. Adam also knew Coach oversaw the quarterbacks and took great pride in their development. He produced winners both on the field and in life. The expectations of a quarterback in this system were lofty and almost always fully accomplished within the four years of high school by each quarterback in the system.

During this early game in Adams career, a key moment unfolded. Towards the end of the half, the offense was in hurry-up mode as they were driving, and time was running out. Adam went back to pass, the defense rushed heavily and sacked him 10 yards deep. Now understand, Coach's quarterbacks are taught to get up from the sack and quickly be ready for the next play. They were leaders and thinkers. Move on to the next play with grace and confidence. It is difficult to know the cause of the sack as it could have been a great defensive play, a breakdown of assignments by the linemen, or the wrong reaction from the quarterback (QB). It is difficult for a high school quarterback to quickly assess this and keep the team moving forward. The best response for the quarterback is to keep the offense in moving-forward mode as a team. It also serves to preserve the continuity of the team. No blaming or accusations. After all, there is no "I" in team!

Coach also pointed out to his quarterbacks during their first day of practice each year an imperative for their survival. Coach understood each of his QBs had enough ego to want the success of their team and to be the QB of such a team. Knowing their goals, they also had to each take on the role of a confident and non-emotional leader on the field. No outward out of control actions, no inspiring head-banging speeches seen in movies, and no goofy "follow me into the battle, boys" attitude. Coach M explained they must set a goal to be the encourager and ultimate calming force on the field. After having coached football, I can understand this request. Coach simply told them if they can't find a way to be this type of QB, then they needed to find a new role on the team. They would not serve the team well without this request being fulfilled. Now this did not mean getting off the team if they did not fit the role. It was a simple requirement of the job and the team. Those young men's role on the team was first defined by their personal goals and attributes. If it fit, they found their role. If it did not fit, then their role needed to be a different one on the team.

As we join Adam back on the field, remember he is about to get up from being tackled behind the line of scrimmage late in that first half. The reaction he began to display did not fulfill the expectation of grace and confidence. He reacted with anger and disgust, yelling at his offensive linemen about their ability. Time started clicking away, the offense was out of sorts, and the half ended without them getting another shot at scoring with a pass into the end zone. Understand, Coach rarely screamed at his young men. He was firm, but rarely was critical of a player who was genuinely making an effort. "Correct and coach" was his mentality. Adam's reaction was a complete breakdown of the process and protocol he knew was expected. And he soon found out how severe.

As the rest of the team had the beginning of their halftime discussions and adjustments with the coaching staff, Adam had a different experience. He was taken aside by Coach, who, although shorter than Adam, started a conversation within a foot or so of Adam's face. As Coach tells me, it was a clear moment of Adam making a conscious decision as to whether his goals were appropriate for the role he chose to play on the team. Coach was not about to allow a single reaction to destroy the team environment he had built. Players were not to be demeaned on his watch. Not by him, his coaches, or other players.

Adam was talented, and many would argue he had exceptional talent. Many coaches would hesitate to address Adam so clearly and definitively. There would be a fear of having Adam walk off. Coach was not concerned with that potential outcome. He understood each person fits a role on the team. Each person's role must align with their abilities and personal goals. Each of his players was a valuable team member. However, if the role a team member plays does not align with their personal goals and vision, then, as leader, Coach M needed to address the situation.

As Coach tells me, Adam was not meant to feel like a

failure. He was firmly told his personal reaction was not going to allow for success in his role in the future. This behavior was not associated with the team he chose to be a part of. He was also asked if he understood and still wanted to be a part of the team in his current role. Although other players likely saw Adam and Coach having a one-sided butt chewing, Coach and Adam knew differently. Adam had reacted in a disparate manner to his earlier discussion with Coach at the beginning of the season. He knew it. He also heard Coach explain a core value was to never be critical of another player's performance during a game. That lesson may have been delivered a little more succinctly! Nonetheless, it was a great example of the connection between the "M" and "E" in team and the concept of no "I."

As I said earlier, spending a short time with Coach was the equivalent of a four-year degree in life skills. Ultimately, Coach explained to me that Adam went on to have a successful football and high school career. I am not sure how Adam would have told the story. My guess is that his version would have been similar to Coach's version, as he would not likely have had the success he had without a complete appreciation for the lesson's learned.

Most successful coaches who deal with team understand the "M" and "E" in team, even if not fully recognized in words or actions. Often, we hear any sort of team leader talk about keeping the team's focus and not letting their minds drift. We also hear about keeping the environment, or culture, positive. These are all statements and beliefs about having a synchronized group of teammates both as a team and individually. The mindset and the environment we are working within are vital for success.

Another way to understand "the 'ME' in team" is to

think of the two letters as representing the words *Mind* and *Environment.* While running competitively a number of years ago, I experienced this concept. Any type of individual sport can be a lonely and intimidating environment to place oneself in. After experiencing many ups and downs, I quickly learned I was the only person who could control the thoughts and concepts in my mind. As well, I was best served to accomplish my goals by surrounding myself with those who had similar goals and priorities to mine.

Of course, reading this book so far (or at least skimming because someone bought it for you or you were misguided enough to buy it on with your own free will, so you want your value), it is obvious the environment I am talking about is not the atmospheric conditions or smog report on the nightly news. Environment is the aspects of the culture each of us strives to attain. The word *culture* is used so often in our world. During the writing of this book, I often find myself exploring the definitions of words. My wife often reminds me how I can carve up the standards of appropriate use of the English language. She is right and I thank God for sending her to me for many reasons. Her use and knowledge of the English language being one of the bonuses I get for having her a part of my life.

As I looked up the words *culture* and *environment,* it is easy to the see the common threads I am referring to. Webster's Dictionary defines *environment* as "the circumstances, objects, or conditions by which one is surrounded." I love this definition, as it speaks to the essence of the concept of "ME."

However, first we must accept we have control over our thoughts and feelings swirling around inside ourselves. It is not always easy and simplistic to have control of those thoughts. We are bombarded with outside images and concepts, causing a veering of the pathway of thought we want to take. I would assert it is tough for a young person living in a world of poverty and strife to be able to focus on becoming a citizen of significant impact in a high-powered career. Their thoughts are often on survival and a path forward to a life of less struggles for daily basic needs.

On the other side of the equation is the person who has been blessed to live in a world of significant wealth and access to resources. This young person can see the path forward to many opportunities, and their mind is focused on accomplishment and not daily basic need struggles. My instinct at this point is to get on my soapbox and preach on how to fix this dilemma in society. I will spare all the brilliance of that rant for a later book. However, it does illustrate how difficult it can be to control the aspects of our thoughts and the "mind." It took me significant time to write the last few paragraphs as my focus was shifted to community issues.

It is also an appropriate point of our time together to appreciate the difficulties each of us face in controlling our thoughts. Most likely, all of us have heard by simply repeating a concept or word in our minds on a repetitive basis every day, the concept or action those words suggest will become part of our subconscious reactions to the world around us. This makes sense. As well, for the person stuck in an environment of negativity with no path forward, the repetitive thoughts of that culture become their personal thoughts. It becomes very difficult to control the thoughts we most want to emulate without having identified or experienced the potential outcomes of those thoughts or pathways in life.

This is where mind and environment connect. Recognition of the need to separate from or actively adjust an environment to move forward with a specific definition of success is hard work. There are countless examples of great and famous leaders changing the direction of organizations by changing the mind and the environmental factors. Just as previously discussed, many of the actions these leaders take allow for members of their teams to self-select in or out of the team. When there is not an alignment with personal and professional goals and priorities, the team will not reach the ultimate level of success. The minds of each team member need to align with the environment the team operates in.

Let me provide a great story of such a journey.

The story begins with a school principal we will call Dr. A. He was assigned to a school of 7th, 8th, and 9th graders in a metropolitan area. The school sat in the middle of a largely low to middle income area. It was a tough time for this area as factories had been closing in this community, economic conditions were difficult throughout the state, and the attitudes of families were deteriorating. Of course, this has an impact on the students walking through the doors of any such school.

However, there were many positive aspects of the culture. There was a diversity (although limited) in the student population, a significant pride in the community, and strong religious or faith-based organizations throughout the school's geographic footprint. The sense of family was present and there were parents willing to work hard to improve the future for their kids. Also, there was little judgement of one another within the community. As we may say today, "you be you." As long as we are all working for the betterment of our community, we can get along was a genuine sentiment of this community.

Dr. A understood these factors in a more significant manner than anyone. This understanding allowed him to see the disconnect with specific faculty members who focused on the negative aspects of the school. These negatively oriented staff members had become leaders in the mindset of the school. Although principals prior to Dr. A had tried to address the school's issues, the environment within the walls of the school needed change. It was assumed by some of the teachers that because these were not students of financial means, often "just a factory worker's son or daughter," the pathway for such students was predetermined. Dr. A could see this language and attitude had become accepted behavior by some.

The predetermined path was to always be in the same culture as their parents. Unfortunately, these same teachers felt the parents were less than who they were as teachers. This attitude became all too prevalent within the school. That thinking allowed for food fights in cafeterias on a regular basis, thuggish behavior in the hallways, and general despair. Athletic teams rarely won games as the mindset was assumed to be "we don't have the resources to compete."

Great coaches and teachers were not supported by the culture of the school, so there was little accountability for achieving success. The vocal and destructive small group of staff influenced the mindset and environment of the school. When Dr. A entered the building as the new leader, the acceptance of a changing world with limited hope was about to become the pathway for choosing growth. Those not on board were soon going to find themselves in conflict with a new mindset and environment.

Dr. A began to change the environment for the school from day one. The culture became one of winning. Winning was defined as setting and achieving goals to improve the lives of students, impact the community and excel as a school staff.

We all like to win and have achievement. Academics suddenly became the focus, as teachers were not allowed to accept lack of effort from students. The excuse from staff members who said "it is just who these kids are," was removed from the discussions. Dr. A held teachers accountable for each lesson every day of the week.

Parents were communicated with and encouraged to be as involved in the school as they could. Athletic facilities were cleaned up and fundraising for new facilities began. Parents had a say in the school, and they took ownership of areas they could. Those parents who saw a new positive team effort were identified and eventually became the leaders of a new approach. There were confrontations with Dr. A and parents, as he did not waiver from his core beliefs. However, his openness and communication allowed for an opportunity for growth with each change all faced. And now the parents were part of identifying the changes, both good and bad, and finding growth pathways.

Soon, the results started producing a new winning attitude defining the new environment. In a few years, test scores went up. Teachers who wanted to be in this new environment stayed and recruited others. Teachers not wanting to be in this new world were now in shrinking number and less vocal than in the past. The team now had a mindset defined by encouraging each student to become their best version of themselves.

The momentum built to a crescendo during a multi-year run of extraordinary accomplishment. The 9th-grade football program completed back-to-back straight conference titles, losing only one game in that two-year span. All football teams from 7th-9th grades had winning seasons and record numbers of students participating. Wrestling teams had conference titles, the track program saw multiple successes at all levels. Band and choirs produced all city music award winners and went on to great success at the high school level. All fine art programs became a source of pride, as concerts and plays were heavily attended. Showing up early to concerts became imperative if one wanted to get a seat in the auditorium, as events were packed.

The thoughts of the parents and students were of accomplishment. There was now pride in the school and a lasting impact on their neighborhoods and community. The evidence was reflected with trophy cases getting filled, coaches and teachers leading with distinction, and parental engagement.

If you ask Dr. A, he will tell you of the greatest symbol of his change in the "ME" of the community. It was a cream-colored carpet in a cafetaria. Back in the days when he took over and there were multiple food fights in the cafeteria, the two cafeterias they had were not in the best shape. They were old marble floors and the walls looked weathered. There was one cafeteria that could be fully seen by many visitors to the school as it also housed the concession stand for extra circular activities. No doors to shut off, just full visibility to all. The room hosted lunch, small school events, and banquets of celebration.

As Dr. A immediately started to fix the discipline issues, he assigned an associate principal who focused on just the discipline issue. The cafeterias were a central element of holding students accountable for their actions. Soon, there were extra staff at every lunch period, and anyone caught not abiding by the defined code of conduct was disciplined according to the rules. The entire school was run this way. The lunchroom was no exception.

His goal was to install a cream-colored carpet in the cafeteria exposed to public viewing. Yes, cream-colored carpet with

7th, 8th, and 9th graders! The symbolism of keeping such a room so clean and the patrons so proud to "own" the beauty of the room would be the shining moment of the new approach. The results of a new mind and environment would be displayed as a permanent pattern of success for all to see.

He installed the carpet and paid for it with fundraising money students and parents worked towards. When he began the remodeling of the room, friends of Dr. A from around the school district laughed and told him the carpet would only last a year. Several years later, with the same creamy white carpet still in place, he hosted a meeting of principals from the district in the room. The "ME" of his world was a success. He had started with "ME" in building his team and kept building from there.

He would later go on to accomplish this again in another school before retiring. Many of his former teachers became administrators inspired by his example. His students always respected his plan, even when they did not like the discipline and structure. Students experienced results they could not achieve without his process.

Often this story has popped into my mind during my time of diagnosis of Parkinson's. It would greatly impact how I would build my team. There is no "I" in team. In my view of the concept and word of *team*, there are several "I's," each uniquely positioned to make a uniform pronunciation of the mission of each team. Without those individuals there is just one person trying to rally an uncoordinated effort. Not a team.

SEVEN

WISDOM

VOLUMES AND VOLUMES of books exist on the concept of wisdom. We use the word constantly. We readily throw out the compliment of wisdom. One could argue it is often overused and not usually understood. Before being diagnosed with Parkinson's, I often spoke on the subject of wisdom. Giving examples and telling stories, I defined wisdom as the ability to incorporate knowledge, information, personal experience, and the experience of others to make more informed decisions in the present and future. I believed in, but never fully comprehended, the importance of wisdom until I heard, "You have Parkinson's."

When adversity comes speeding down the pathway of personal or organizational life, we are all good at attaching catchy phrases and strategies we have heard from others. All are well intentioned. Many have great and impactful meaning. Each nugget of information we can dig up during times to address adversity has value. It is not just the knowledge from one nugget of information or catchy phrase which can have significance on us personally or on our work life. It is the accumulation of this massive body of information, knowledge, and experience from the world around us where the most impact on our decisions is gained.

Do we understand this concept consciously? Not likely. As mentioned earlier, we occasionally just hit societal default answers and move on, thinking we have overcome the adversity. Not a great answer for having the most impact on a mission and vision. Unfortunately, likely the answer too many choose. After all, it is difficult to hit Ctrl+Alt+Del. It requires attention and thought. Once we do hit reset, who knows what is on the other side of the task manager we are exploring in life. Scary stuff!

Knowledge and information are interrelated concepts. Wisdom relies upon them both. We all have basic information on the world around us. Facts, figures, basic truths we are taught. We are given tests on our knowledge of information and facts on a regular basis. We learn information and facts constantly. This knowledge and information provide us with awareness of the situation we may be facing.

The ability to apply our knowledge to a specific situation we are faced with is the process of making informed decisions. Each time the situation or circumstances change in front of us, we start pulling in experiences we have had. We continue to apply those experiences to our knowledge and information database to execute more informed decisions. It is a constant process our brain executes for us.

When I think of the wisest people I have ever met, or study the wisest of companies, there is a distinct difference in their application of wisdom to their worlds. The wisest among us apply the experiences of not just themselves, but of those around them. This extension of their database of information and knowledge provides for the greatest potential of successful outcomes. With their expanded database, they can transact a more complete and informed decision-making process. They have achieved the highest level of wisdom they can possibly reach at a specific and particular point in time. Most importantly, the wisest individuals and companies have learned to complete this decision-making process instinctively. They formed a controlled response to change with a wise decision-making process.

Let's take an example from my journey of Parkinson's. I knew what Parkinson's was from a basic perspective. I had experienced folks who have it. My family doctor as a child had PD later in life. Seeing him during his retirement, after he had been diagnosed, I could not help but feel sad for him. He had been one of the greatest family practice doctors in my city. He seemed frustrated and frail. That was similar to the other experiences I had with the disease.

There was also the basic information on Parkinson's I was familiar with prior to diagnosis. Those pieces included that it was neurological, progressive, tremors and not much else. My knowledge was limited. Having watched a friend and a few others I know lose their battles with ALS and MS, I knew any of the symptoms of the neurological disease category were not good or desirable.

However, there was a significant gap in my information and the subsequent knowledge of how the disease works. I discovered this abruptly. As I began to understand the defining factors of Parkinson's, I realized how much I did not know. For example, each person's journey can be drastically and radically different. Symptoms are all similar in form, but manifest themselves at different times, stages, and outcomes throughout the life of a PD patient. This was a mind-blowing phenomenon to me. How could we (meaning society) not understand this disease any better than this? Why have we not gained more knowledge than this? The answer is complex, of course. It is also understandable as I became more knowledgeable about the facts and figures of PD.

In order to have the full ability to make informed decisions about my care and future, I needed to understand the entire picture. Soon, I learned I needed wisdom. Remember, I define wisdom as the ability to incorporate knowledge, information, personal experience, and the experience of others to make more informed decisions in the present and future. The experiences and decisions others had made regarding their Parkinson's treatment were to be significant data points for me. It allowed me to make the most informed and appropriate decisions. My quest was to gain the needed information, knowledge, and experience of others to make more informed decisions for me and my family. This is engagement in a wise decision-making process.

Wisdom takes time to develop. When we are younger, we rely more on the experiences of others to impact our decisions. If we are wise at an early age, we are taking the experiences of those around us to impact our own lives in a positive manner. As we age, our own experiences tend to replace those of others. It is often difficult to ascertain if decisions are made with the experience shared from others or personal wisdom. The process hopefully becomes seamless. Nonetheless, wisdom does not usually come at an early age.

We often miss opportunities to mature into wise decision makers. The experiences we see from others may have been framed in ways confusing for us due to the labels attached. Society tells us to not pay attention to the "loser" or the "failed leader." However, all these experiences are relevant if we are to gain complete wisdom. I have seen this firsthand in my PD experience. A decision to take a specific pharmaceutical may have been a great decision for one patient, but horrific for another. If I was to be able to decipher the experience into wise choices, I needed to understand all the facts of all experiences I could gain. Then apply those facts and experience to my situation. I could not afford to miss an opportunity to gain more knowledge and information. Even those experiences disguised as failures of others were now a vital part of the process. No missed opportunities to learn from.

Unfortunately for me and all PD patients, wisdom is a quick moving target. The medicines change, the information on medicines is evolving, the treatments have success and failure, new scientific connections to old issues arise, a manifestation of research falls short of expectations, and the list goes on. Early on in my PD journey, I once communicated the desire to have the power of a decoder ring—a superpower if I may. This decoder ring could assess information and provide the needed decision points to use the information charting the best course for me. Of course, everyone who has ever gone through a life-altering medical diagnosis has felt something similar. Now I know this. No clue prior to going through the process for myself. I needed firsthand experience combined with others' experience to completely understand the need for the decoder ring to gain wisdom in this quickly changing environment.

It likely seems to the reader of this average book the concept of Ctrl+Alt+Del is overused. That could be correct. However, it will continue to pop up. Having the ability to reset when faced with great and significant change cannot be emphasized enough in words. After going through the first three or so years of my life with a PD diagnosis, I cannot imagine not being able to hit Ctrl+Alt+Del. Being able to assess the needed information of my own life, researching facts, and learning from others to make a more informed decision about the present and future was one of the factors allowing me to keep moving forward.

At first, I thought I was unique in my situation in life. Of course, that is true on many levels. We are all unique and have different, distinct lives. Looking deeper into the quest for information, I discovered companies and individuals have been going through this process in their own ways for all of eternity. Each of us, including me, is not alone. Nor is each organization or person the first to be forced to choose a path forward. (OK, it is appreciated that somebody had to be the first, but that is a debate for a different kind of book.) Knowing these facts, one had to conclude feeling sorry for myself because I was the only one to face such an issue was not a path forward. Darn! If only we could all just claim self-pity and get a free pass to a more peaceful stage of our personal or our company's journey.

During my first few years of Parkinson's, I had the pleasure to have a brief but significant exchange with a former Navy SEAL. We were able to exchange a few e-mails and I also had a conversation with his father. Retiring from the SEALs is not a normal retirement. The job they perform during their career is unthinkable to any of us who are not one of them or command them. Our country will be forever in debt to such amazing men and women. Thank you!

During my exchange with him, his e-mail to me was simple

and profound. I had asked for time to talk with him as I was researching stories of success for my speaking opportunities and a potential book. I missed our first chance to talk via phone due to a medical issue. In the follow-up e-mails, his response was one of the best examples of wisdom and defining success one could imagine. Coming home from the military and adapting to life as a civilian is difficult for those with military careers. It is typically even more difficult when you perform the duties of a SEAL. This, we can all agree, is a fact.

During his response to me, he merely stated he was not sure why he was significant in my research. When others his age were at the peak of their earning potential, he chose to live a more meaningful life with his own business. He was happy with his wife and children, fulfilled with his work, and looked forward to getting out of bed every day. It is simple: he had made an informed and wise decision with his family on their path forward. He could have easily made a lot more money in many different ventures. After talking to others, learning of their experiences, and assessing his life, his path had to be his own. I have intentionally left out details of my interactions with him to protect his identity. He and his wife will recognize this reference. Thank you!

Examples abound all around us of those facing great times of adversity and change. Each example also illustrates an attempt to choose growth through wisdom. I am an advocate for an increased awareness of the importance of mental health. Getting rid of the stigma of mental illness needs to keep moving forward. It is a great example of how a lack of facts can lead to a lack of wise decision making. Often, stories of suicide have been preceded with a lack of understanding as to the severity of mental disease. This lack of knowledge and experience, combined with the lack of sharing of experiences, has led us to not treat mental disease with the needed transparency it requires.

In 2008, we faced a severe financial crisis in America with the housing bubble. Anyone living through it certainly appreciates the crisis and its outcomes on America. For those not of age to be aware of this time, go back and study it. It is a great example of leaders searching for wisdom. We heard references to past crises and the government's response in the news. We watched as friends and relatives tried to understand the best pathway for them to sustain themselves with information difficult to grasp. Home values dropping by historic numbers, foreclosures skyrocketing, and bankruptcies escalating. All wanted to have wisdom, taking into account the past successes and failures as best they could. Everyone needed wisdom.

Start-up companies are always in need of wisdom. With no experience as an organization, they rely upon the individuals' collective information, knowledge, and experience to create a wise path to success. Many successful start-ups hire experienced CEOs coupled with young, smart staff. The young staff often have cutting-edge knowledge and skill sets to greatly impact an industry. The experienced CEO has the ability to filter through the vast amount of data points to make informed decisions on strategies needed to survive.

The opposite of this is all around us. The dot-com bubble is a great example. Although there were many reasons why this bubble caused many to lose their jobs and life savings, lack of wisdom was among them. There were many companies starting up with experience and confidence from one previous success. They had experience from one source, knowledge of products and needed services, and dedicated, smart teams.

However, there were countless stories of leadership in these firms having all the tech and internet knowledge they needed to succeed, but who would not learn from the failures or successes of previous ventures. So many times, we saw leadership teams who were successful with one startup quickly branch out again. Unfortunately, many of those follow up companies were followed with a major disaster. Often, they had used the same formula as their prior successful company was built upon. Big mistake, as the world was changing around them. The identical formula will not work with different circumstances. It also assumes the previous formula was perfect with no hiccups the first time. Ha! Wisdom was not present.

Generational businesses often fall victim to the lack-of-wisdom mistake. How many times have we witnessed the second- or third-generation owners discovering the formula for success is not working? Often, the first generation did not arrive at the formula for success without learning from their own and others' experiences. I have had countless business owners tell me of their success after watching and learning from a competitor's failure. They apply the concept of wisdom to their business. This extends the life of their business. However, in second or third generation businesses, the experiences and wisdom can become watered down or don't get passed along with the proper context.

One of the greatest examples of a wise approach to an industry is the trade unions. Most, if not all, trade unions have apprenticeship programs. They combine the basics of learning a trade in a classroom-type setting with the practical application of the knowledge while on the job with an experienced mentor. The apprentice combines their own experience, information, and knowledge with the experience of a veteran in their trade. This formula leads to confident and independent apprentice graduates ready to start and advance in their work on their own. Contractors will affirm they could not survive without such great programs. When interacting with a skilled tradesperson, notice the amazing level of confidence and skill. Well-executed program of wisdom. One that should be considered and modeled upon in several other industries struggling to find new contributors to their ranks.

Thinking through my diagnosis of PD and the subsequent adventure is the culmination of the concept of wisdom for me. I had talked about wisdom and all of its components for years. Now, I was living it. After spending time understanding the basic information and knowledge, I then had to move forward with experience from the others around me. It was not always easy for me. Accepting and acknowledging the need for other's skills, information and experience is humbling and downright scary. It still is not easy. Each day I think about the need for greater wisdom. I meditate on it and remind myself of the needed skills to keep living my best life. Nobody ever said the pursuit of wisdom is supposed to be easy.

EIGHT

—✥—

ADAPT. ADJUST. REPEAT.

WISDOM IS A concept we need for our entire life. Of course, it is. As I stated early and often in this book, change is inevitable all around us. Each of us, individually or organizationally, is forced to change every day. Never have I experienced this more than in the two years prior to and three years following my diagnosis. Attempting to make wise decisions each day has also taught me the importance of the ability to adapt and adjust.

As discussed briefly in the last chapter, successful people and organizations are lifelong learners. They accept that change is inevitable and look for the path of growth in the current situation. I think I have played that tune a few times in this book! All too often, however, we struggle to adapt our plan to the situation we are given and adjust our goals to what is happening in front of us. Or in some cases, it takes a long time to realize adjustments need to be made. We often forget learning is a lifelong pursuit.

It may appear odd to say in some ways, but I have been lucky and blessed in life. Not in getting PD. I am pretty confident that was not a lucky diagnosis. However, I was fortunate in having the needed skills and background to recognize the game had changed for me. No longer was I planning for a healthy and long retirement as my option. That is no longer a dream I could afford to live within. Oh sure, advancements may come along and allow me to enjoy life to the extent I would have once planned for in my later years. Nothing will be ruled out in my hopes and dreams. However, it would be irresponsible for me to have future medical advancements as my primary plan for the future. Future medical advancements as a primary plan would be the equivalent of completing an annual personal budget and entering "lottery winnings" under the income section. Unless the winning ticket has already been cashed, it is not likely a good plan. I have been lucky, but not "lottery" winnings lucky.

Once I knew I needed to adapt and adjust my plan, the next steps became more difficult. This was already discussed in detail for those who have made it this far in the book. After making the needed adjustments to my future thoughts, I then had to actually transact each step of the future plan. I needed to complete detailed financial planning to include items such as long-term care scenarios, potential for disability, and planning for my wife to be on her own when I pass. Making adjustments such as these were difficult in many ways.

The planning process also became a part of the overall process of moving forward. At times, I was good at embracing the planning process. At times, I wanted to scream and just drink myself into a state of not caring. In a quest for knowledge, I have talked to many others who have been diagnosed with Parkinson's or other life altering and shortening diseases. These conversations were held both prior to and after my diagnosis. Those conversations have provided great insights. Unfortunately, it is all too easy to avoid the planning and moving forward process by finding alternatives such as alcohol and other substances. That plan is not a way to find growth and move forward.

Most of us have had plans interrupted at some point in life. The same is true of business. We plan a night out, a weekend of fun, a big move across the country, starting a new business, our retirement, and the list goes on. No matter the size or scope, rarely does the plan work out exactly as forecasted. Interruptions also come in all shapes, sizes and sometimes disguises. In whatever form they present themselves, these interruptions are real and must be dealt with. Ignoring the interruption is a choice. It takes control out of the hands of those most impacted and delivers control to others. Companies make this mistake often. When they do, they allow their competitors to control their own destiny. Then a small interruption to the goals or strategy becomes a full-scale crisis. Acknowledging the interruptions is key to moving forward.

After I was diagnosed with PD, I experienced euphoria in a unique manner. I had finally figured out the issue I was dealing with and the possibilities for adjusting my life were endless. At that particular moment in time, I was shocked, disappointed, and scared, but the opportunity to find growth was endless. I received countless words of advice and consultation. Although occasionally extremely off base, the sentiment was genuine and heartfelt. This experience happens to us all when going through tremendous change. This is especially true of individuals and companies navigating through times of extreme positive opportunity. We all want to be excited about potential or actual winning!

After three or four months, I began to understand the opportunity more deeply for growth in my life. I had begun to lose the weight I had gained. I was working out almost daily and starting to feel a minimal amount of improvement in my health. This likely allowed me to think outside of the basic survival instincts. Again, this is similar to companies adapting after going through huge negative dips. Once an organization has started to navigate towards a measurable positive result, it becomes easier to dig deeper into the future state, leaving behind the uncertainty.

There was another feeling often in my daily life. I was also experiencing the real sense of loss and grief that comes with this horrible disease. I saw the disappointment and fear of the situation with my wife and children. It was complicated as I began seeing how my friends and coworkers handled news of this type as well. I found myself in a reflective mood quite often. Nonetheless, I was slowly starting to deal with the adjustments in my life. Essentially, I was moving through the grieving process.

Whether I was consciously aware or not, I was beginning to experience a similar process we all take on as our plans are changed or interrupted. We evaluate the facts, adapt our perception of the reality we are experiencing, and adjust our strategies moving forward. Hopefully, we are using a pathway of wisdom and educated decision making. Each of us or our organizations we work within gathers the new facts in a variety of manners. Wise people and companies rely upon a comprehensive evaluation of the knowledge, information, and experience to make informed decisions on the present and future. Often, there is a reliance on the same pattern, skill set or strategies once successful. It is easy to fall into this trap.

Examples are all around us of dependence of similar pathways of success to be applied to evolving, new facts of our lives. There is the athlete who was great at in-game decisions and adjustments. Their preparation and muscle memory for these decisions have made them seem calm and in control. They are lauded with praise for their ability and game-time skill. Then, the athletic career is over, and the next chapter in life begins. The next chapter requires them to focus on preparation, planning, and skill development. They likely perfected this process with practice and performed in a game-time setting. However, life is an ongoing process that may not have an exact score, time clock and finality. An adjustment needs to occur in applying the great preparation and skills once learned in athletics to the world of business. Many have failed to reach the same heights in life they achieved in athletics. We have all seen it.

The example of the star athletes also sheds light on sports. There are sports analogies tossed around in business and often used to an extreme. The references can be found quite often in the newest, greatest books hitting the market. And we all must read these books to be successful. However, these references are just analogies. They are not goals, and often don't contain any strategy applicable to living outside of a game. Most organizations and people are not measured with a perfect four-quarter game with a winner and trophy each day. However, there is once similarity. Both games and life outside of a game require adjustment, adaption and implementation of the adapted plan.

Then, repeat as often as needed.

I have an estimated 90 percent usage of the right side of my body compared to my left. This was the evaluation at the time of the original diagnosis. In essence, my PD was attacking my right side first. This is common in Stage One of PD. Weakness, tremors, muscle twitches, dystonia, and other symptoms appear in just one side of the body. For me, this was evident. I am also right-handed and use my right arm more than my left. As a result, it was difficult to see the difference in strength change, as my right side is dominant and stronger. So, working on the development of my right and left sides of the body in uniformity was key.

In the earlier days of my life, I was known as having great flexibility. Partially due to stretching, but also due to having rather "loose joints." Sounds great as a youth and an athlete. Not such a good thing in the long term. I sprain ankles, twist knees, and tear body parts up with great ease. Now imagine having the effect of Parkinson's when balance and stability become progressively more difficult. I had relied upon my flexibility and loose joints for years. Now I needed to find a way to strengthen every muscle in the body affecting my balance. Which leads me to my next revelation from being slapped with Parkinson's diagnosis.

It also became evident in my early days of diagnosis of the overreliance many people and companies have upon a core strength. This often leads to the underdevelopment of other skills. Those underdeveloped skills lead to the issue of unbalance and a lack of stability. Unlike the athlete I mentioned earlier who just may not translate the right skills into nonathletic ventures in life, organizations and people often "overplay" their best skills in life without developing others.

This over reliance on a core skill works to a certain extent.

For example, the guitar player who has amazing dexterity for the strings can make a career out of it. However, eventually the dexterity lessens. The ability for the same musician to understand the music at a deeper level and hear the sound more succinctly now becomes as important as the feel for the strings and the instrument. But what do most do? That's right, we emphasize dexterity and run with the wind at our back, letting the dexterity carry us long and far. Ride that great core skill set until it can't be ridden any more.

Companies do this constantly. The tech sector is famous for it. We have had dotcom and tech bubbles in the last 20 years in America and much of the rest of the world. Now these bubbles are caused by many factors. It is naive to not see the over-reliance on specific strengths and ignoring of weaknesses as one of the fundamental causes of the dotcom bubble. Companies took venture capital and kept hiring programmers and coders, instead of strong accountants and business planners to prepare the business for the future. There was a race to the future of the next greatest breakthrough, accentuating the skill sets of speed and endurance. 70-hour work weeks, stock options rather than salary, more venture capital to stay ahead of the competition rather than generating revenue from the current solution. Eventually, the world changes. Economies contract, political winds turn, and good workers become exhausted with the wait for their company to go public to "cash in."

One or any combination of such events can and did cause massive negative disruption to organizations. The overreliance upon the strengths of "just get this product to market" mentality certainly played into bubbles bursting. Long-term planning had been ignored by many in the tech and dotcom world. When the bubble burst, there was nothing to fall back upon.

Overemphasizing one core strength often causes a blind spot for identifying multiple other opportunities for growth. Thus, there is not likely balance and stability as a foundation for the future.

For just a minute, we should evaluate personal relationships in life. Friendships built on a single point of common ground do not often stand the test of time. And of course, I have a story about this observation. Years ago, I participated in a leadership program. It was a great issues-based education experience for leaders in Iowa known as Leadership Iowa. I developed many friends in the nine months of the program, as we met once a month for two days. We shared experiences, opinions, meals, a beverage or two, and dove deep into the issues of our state. Each year, as these sessions end, the current group of participants discuss how they will stay in touch and become lifelong business associates and/or friends. However, experience indicates most only stay in touch with a few of their leadership classmates beyond just a few years. The intentions are good. There appears to be such common ground, but for many the common ground was just the attendance of the class. The intensity of these sessions is a great example of a false sense of deep personal connections. Please don't misunderstand. The relationships developed in this type of format have long lasting tennacles and are invaluable. Those connections one makes that are of the deeper level are irreplaceable.

In order to develop deeper connections with those relationships, there had to be an additional and specific pathway of each relationship. An additional set of commonalities was needed outside of just the common ground of the monthly classes. A charitable cause, common business interests, geographic interests, common background, common friends, or relationship circles. These commonalities have allowed me to further develop relationships with specific members of the leadership class. In essence, each relationship I have developed had a complexity of not just emphasizing the common and intense experience of Leadership Iowa. There was a needed effort or development of multiple components to drive a successful relationship. It was not just a reliance on the dominant strength of attendance to monthly sessions.

As a side note, anyone who may get the opportunity to experience a program such as Leadership Iowa, should not just walk through the door. They should run as fast as they can through the door. No matter the age or background of the participant, learning from others in this type of setting is invaluable.

As I began to experience my new life with PD, I was constantly struggling to set goals around my disease state. I still face the same struggle to this day. Early, I found the strength to complete long workouts and strength-building sessions. I was seeing progress. Then, about 12 months into my diagnosis, the chronic pain was starting to wear me down. Mind over matter can only last so long. They increased my dosages of medications. Unfortunately, those adjustments caused side effects and fatigue. Abdominal issues and severe "off periods" were just too much. At 12–18 months into my diagnosis, I was on track in preparation for several distance-type athletic events. My first was going to be a triathlon. Or so I thought.

By this time, I had ramped up my public speaking and established a new website and approach to my keynote presentations. I was determined to tell the world the story of change is inevitable, and growth is optional. Appearing at Parkinson's and corporate events, there was a pathway to grow from this seemingly bad situation. Privately, I was suffering. My symptoms were not improving, and a new team of doctors took over in November of 2018. The result was an adaptation to my plans of distance athletic events and feats of endurance. With this change, I had to adapt my speaking and presentation schedule. Adjustment, adaptation, repeat.

Over the next several months, there was the adjustment to new medications and the side effects from them. The medications caused severe nausea and often gagging and vomiting. Each morning was a wild card as to whether the taste of toothpaste was going to make me throw up, gag, or just go about my day with no issues. More often than not, I was gagging and vomiting each day. This caused stomach and esophagus issues. I had to limit alcohol consumption, as it usually made me throw up the next day, even if I only had just one or two drinks. All the fun of a hangover, with none of the relaxing effect of a few drinks.

All of this meant my exercise routines needed adaptation. It was kind of tough to focus on long methodical workouts when halfway through I would have to stop and gag! My goals changed. I could no longer rely upon my strengths from endurance events.

I also started to experience greater dystonia. Dystonia is a cramping-type sensation that occurs in the body. For me, my feet and legs experience this. Combined with my chronic pain, it creates fun days. Shorter, more intense workouts became the best way for me to deal with my symptoms. As well, I was now focusing on exercise to maintain balance and stability more than ever. These workouts alleviated the negative effects of the dystonia.

Just like in life before Parkinson's, there was the cycle of adapting, adjusting, and repeating about every six months. It is unclear to me if I consciously recognized the cycle of these six-month changes. However, I clearly had found a rhythm. This is similar to any person or organization: adapt and adjust. The constantly changing world forces us to do so. Also, we may not even recognize we are adapting and adjusting. It just occurs as a result of intuitive skill development. It is similar to a conditioned response. Change occurs, we find a new pathway for growth, and the cycle continues.

Now, as many of us experience, adaptation does not always come easy. I resisted the shorter, more succinct workouts. Then I discovered I could start doing shorter sprinting workouts on the track. They exhilarated me. I even thought about trying to start competing in master track. The thought of an old (51-year-old at the time), bald, five-foot-eleven-inch, 205-pound man with occasional balance issues running 100- to 800-meter intervals on the track should create a picture of humor. I will admit, I am relatively lean and strong for a man my age, but it is still a sight nobody should have to watch. In four or five months, there is great progress experienced in this new routine of shorter workouts. These workouts, along with my strength and development work, had me believing competition with others of a similar age was possible. I could show the world the strength of a Parkinson's patient.

This process reminded me of the many companies I have seen undergo the same process. They find a pathway to success, adjust the strategy, but never lose site of the mission and vision of their companies.

Once we make adjustments, it is also a risk that we go back to overreliance on a newly found skill or strength. I proved this risk to be a realized pathway in glaring and glowing fashion.

There I went, overemphasizing a skill set, driving myself to a new pathway without thinking about the other weaknesses I needed to acknowledge. I was sprinting, doing strength training, hitting the swimming pool to rest my legs on specific days. Too much, too soon. Tearing the meniscus of the right knee, surgery was needed. Organizations do the same. If the new product is selling well, let's come out with three similar products and saturate the market. The market gets confused and then all four products fail.

Surgery with Parkinson's is an adventure. As mentioned earlier, I am familiar with surgical procedures. But there were now new considerations: timing of the medicines, not being able to take the pain medications like others, the chronic pain I already was experiencing, and oh yeah … I have tremors. Try administering an IV to a patient with tremors. The surgery went well. I was back training again in 60 days on the treadmill, running short fast workouts. Unfortunately, by this time, winter had arrived in Iowa. There were no outside track workouts. It is tough to run on the track with snow on it! Adjust, adapt, repeat.

This adjusting, adapting and repeating can only be successful if there is commitment to the mission and vision an individual or a company carries. One could say there must be a passionate love for the defined mission and vision.

NINE

LOVE

LOVE IS A big concept.

Webster's Dictionary has two entries for the word *love*, with 13 different definitions and variations. Where does one even begin to discuss such a topic?

One such definition is "to hold dear: cherish." When one is faced with a diagnosis of a life-altering neurological disease, cherishing each day becomes essential. Most of us have discovered the concept of love to mean more than just cherishing.

My journey with change led me to understand the phrase "love like a dog." I know this sounds strange, as a dog is an animal and not a fair comparison to humans. There is also awareness that saying a dog is just an animal offends many. Dogs are more than pets. They are family members, friends, comforters, and more than "just" animals. These facts are the basis of why "loving like a dog" resonates when there is rapid change.

Dogs unload an amazing amount of unconditional love on their owners. Certainly, there are examples of mean or vicious dogs. Those dogs usually had poor owners. Dogs want to love unconditionally. We had a dog in our house during the time of my diagnosis, Gracie. She was 15 pounds, had beautiful white fur, and was a mix of Westie and Poodle. She was an amazing pet for our family for 12 years before she lost her battle with cancerous tumors. She loved us unconditionally. Even when we were not as attentive as we needed to be, she still responded with love minutes later.

Not being a veterinarian, the following observations are only those of a novice. Dogs are habitual creatures, with strong associated memories. Their memories are not like human memories in many ways. They sometimes appear very similar, but they are not. Dogs associate experiences with memory. My dog Gracie knew that when I said the word "treat," she could run to the cupboard housing her treats and get her favorite dog treat. They associate good feelings with their owners. They love them unconditionally, as they don't carry the baggage humans do from past grudges, upset feelings, disappointments, hurt, shame, anger, and the host of other long-term memories we each harbor.

Gracie reacted with joy every night I arrived back home. She would hear my car pull into the garage, go to the steps where she could see me walk in the door at my eye level, and wait. When I opened the door, she sat and waited for me to say hello, with her tail wagging. It did not matter if I was upset with her earlier in the morning, if my day had been bad, if I was in pain or if I'd had the best day of my life. She had an amazing love for the experience of me arriving home and each time was the same experience for her.

Many stories of the unconditional love of a pet have been shared with me over the years at my speaking engagements. One such came on a trip to Washington, D.C. After I spoke, a young lady came up to me after waiting for quite some time for others in front of her to greet me or extend well wishes. During this presentation on leadership, I finished as I often do with a song playing in the background. This time, it was Elton John's Circle of Life from the Lion King movie. The movie and song have tremendous references to leadership, and it is one of my favorites to end a presentation with.

This young lady also had a service dog in training with her. As many of you know, there are great organizations who assist in training these dogs for service members and others needing a professionally trained dog. She mentioned this was a planned trip with her dog to test the dog on it's behavior in airports and other crowded situations. The dog would need to navigate these situations with its future owner. I was moved by her commitment to the project and told her so. She stopped me as I was expressing my gratitude and feelings for her journey.

She pointed out to me the last song I played in my presentation was very timely and emotional for her. She has always been dedicated to her work with dogs, but the song reminded her why. Although there was significance to assisting others with her training, she mentioned her fury trained friend was reminding her of several life lessons. The ability for a pet to be so well trained to "love and obey their owner so significantly," the "dog serves as lifeline." Unconditionally trained love of their role. She pointed out the "Circle of Life" song reminded her of her essential role and to keep moving forward. She was exhausted with the trip thus far but felt inspired by the response of her fury companion and the mission they served together. Pretty tough story to forget and I have often thought about it since.

A short time after being diagnosed, I had a rough day at work while also suffering from an off day with my disease. What I refer to as the double whammy. But when I arrived home late that night, there was Gracie, tail wagging, ready to greet me. For her, it was a time to associate me with good memories or conditioned responses. I looked at her and did not respond as I usually did by saying, "Who is that girl?" She would get excited to hear this and I would quickly follow with, "It's Gracie." Sounds kind of silly as I write it. But that day was just not worthy of any more words. I had traveled extensively across the country while dealing with lots of work-related issues, all the while being in a lot of physical pain. Compounding the experience was a lack of good sleep for days due to the disease. It did not matter to Gracie: she still sat looking at me the same exact habitual way she always did. She did not move until she finally heard her name come from my mouth.

It was at this moment I concluded there are times in life we all need to "love like a dog." Unconditionally forgetting about the baggage of the day, the week, the month, or even a few years, and love the moment. It hit me like a streaking locomotive (that is a train to those from the younger generations) running down a long hill with no brakes. As bad as my day had been, it was over. Now I needed to focus on the love, both the positives and negatives, of the day. Embrace it all and move on. Unconditional love of those around me, the choices of life, and myself. "Love like a dog," no matter what the events.

This lesson has stayed with me often since my diagnosis. Each experience we have is an opportunity to hold dear the lessons associated with the event. The failures, the successes, good

days, bad days, and all the in between events. My appreciation
for life is different than it has ever been. I want to love each day
as if it were my last. I have tried to live like this since watching
Gracie wag her tail, letting me know of her unconditional love.
Each of us can remember a time when this is clearly laid out for
us. In essence, when each of us was similar to the dog trainer
visiting Washington, D.C.

As noted at the beginning of this chapter, love is defined
in many ways. As we think about examples of unconditional
love in our world, we all have witnessed amazing stories. There
are those couples who have been together for 50-plus years,
enduring good and bad alike. We think of the love we feel for
our children and the need to protect them at any cost, even our
own lives. The act of loving one another in a family.

When faced with an amazing amount of change, especially
negative change, it is difficult to embrace our journey as an unconditional love. However, successful organizations and people
do this every day. We often call this dedication to the mission
and vision. It also goes deeper than just words. It becomes an
attitude and a culture shared with all. This cultural belief allows for unconditional passion and love towards the process
and journey.

Earlier in this book we shared the story about Coach and
his amazing career. His ability to face the ups and downs of
his teams is a great example of "love like a dog." His programs
embraced the values he shared with them and seldom waivered.
Unconditional love and passion for the cause of growing young
men into great lifelong community members.

One last story about Coach M. When he was asked about
one of his most successful seasons, he mentioned the team that
finished 3-6. That means 3 wins and 6 losses. Now for a man

with a state title, numerous conference titles and the many accolades mentioned prior, this is surprising.

His explanation of this answer is clearly an example of love and passion. According to him, that team did not have tremendous god given talent. Very small group of kids that had to work extremently hard to just be competitive. Coach could have taken short cuts to his system and implemented new concepts to get the team over 500 and into a playoff spot. That might have worked, but would have short changed those kids on the value of the system and process.

Coach describes the teams work ethic as amazing and relentless. He hoped they would win a game that year. They won three and almost won several others. They were always competitive and maintained their passion for the process. One of his most successful seasons. That is loving your role in life just like a dog loves it owner.

"Loving like a dog" is definitely not a perfect process. Being human and having a subconscious with the baggage of a lifetime or just the current days resentments don't lend themselves to perfect unconditional love. Perfection is always an aspiration but never quite reachable. That is okay. It also does not equate to stopping our journey at any one destination since there is not perfection. Striving towards the perfection of unconditional love must continue. The commitment to "loving like a dog" is the most important step for all of us to find the love in our life.

Along my journey in life, there have been encounters with those shouldering the burden of serious addictions. Addiction is real for so many in our world today. I am not an expert, so please don't hold my statements as the gospel of addictive personalities.

In dealing with my Parkinson's Disease in the early months, I became more familiar with the mindset of addiction. The first round of medications I was on had a side effect of causing a high level of obsessive-compulsive behavior. Luckily for me, I did not really experience a significant part of this side effect. However, others have experienced gambling addictions, alcoholism, and many other similar issues. Knowing this early in my treatment, for several months, I woke up and wondered if today was going to be the day of going off the rails for me. It was an eye-opening experience.

Knowing this, how does someone deal with a serious addiction find passion in their life? One of the many people interviewed with addiction shed light on this subject for me. She spoke confidentially to me about her journey. For her, she finds her passion in how she approaches each day with a love for managing her disease. She strives to love each day without drugs and alcohol. As she described this missionary zeal for each day, it was clear she "loved like a dog." Of course, her life is not perfect every day. Her goal of perfection is real and recognized in her daily actions. She also conveys that many she knows with her same disease work towards a similar approach to managing their lives. They have passion and embrace their journey. Sounds a lot like "loving like a dog."

As a part of managing adversity caused by constant change, it should be clear to all of us the need to embrace others. It is also noted many with difficult diseases to manage seem to express a form of unconditional love for those around them as often as they can. It appears to be an essential piece in managing through adverse change and finding growth.

Love for others. We all need this.

For those not sure of my intention thus far, I am suggesting to "love like a dog" each of the days we have in life. Not an easy task. Not possible either. We are all human, and there will be days when there is not a moment of "cherished experience." However, when the next day arrives, try to be the dog sitting on the steps with the wagging tail. Associate each day with unconditional love. Love of the wisdom gained from the day, including all of the challenges encountered by us or those around us. Embrace the changing world with a choice of growth from each day's adventure. Today and every day going forward should be the best day of life.

Change is inevitable, growth is optional.

www.ingramcontent.com/pod-product-compliance
Lightning Source LLC
Chambersburg PA
CBHW050923260726
48660CB00001B/371